FROM

TO

MOUNTAIN

KENNETH MOORE

PUBLISHED
AT
THE SIGN OF THE WOOLLY LAMB

Catalogue record for this book is available from the British Library

ISBN
0-9554189-0-9   978-0-9554189-0-7
Printed and bound in Great Britain
by
ProPrint, 136 Priory Street,
Carmarthen, SA31 1LR, Wales

Published at the sign of the Woolly Lamb
Papers used are natural recyclable products made from timber grown in sustainable forests

FRONT COVER:
Holme Lode, Holme Fen
Nature Reserve, Cambs.

BACK PLATE:
Sunset over Samson,
Isles of Scilly

BACK COVER:
View towards Garreg
Las and Waun Lefrith

HALF TITLE PAGE:
Crowland High Wash,
Near Wards Farm

TITLE PAGE:
Grongaer Hill, from
Llangathen Village

To
My
Father
Kenneth George Moore
1920 - 2000

With best wishes
John Moore

March 2011

' Oh take me from the busy crowd
I cannot bear the noise
For nature's voice is never loud
I seek for quiet joys'

John Clare {1793 – 1864}

BIOGRAPHICAL NOTES

Kenneth Moore was born in 1947 at Warboys in the then County of Huntingdonshire where several generations of his family have lived and worked in the Fens. Brought up for all of his school years in the nearby city of Peterborough he trained as an architect at Leicester and has since lived and travelled extensively throughout the country. A specialist in historic and vernacular buildings he is now based in West Wales.

Most of his writing has been published in specialist and professional magazines with one extended series entitled 'The Vanishing Vernacular' appearing in Carmarthenshire Life. He has been deeply involved in the Building Preservation Trust movement for some 20 years both in England and Wales being the founder and chairman of the East Shires Building Preservation Trust and the Carmarthenshire Trust and co founder of the Cambridgeshire Trust.

In 2002 he decided to drop his drawing board and tee square for the camera and tripod and concentrate on photography, his 'second subject' whilst training to be an architect.

He is now a freelance photographer specialising in the built heritage, landscapes, contemporary images based on 'sea, sand and rivers' and rail transport based around the movement of stone.

ACKNOWLEDGMENTS

Like most authors I find it impossible to name everyone who has helped and supported me over the time this book has been in the making. To everyone not included by name please accept my sincere thanks.

I am greatly indebted for the advice, assistance and support of Andy Brash, Adrian and Pam at Proprint of Carmarthen without whom the book would not have been possible. The fantastic support and professionalism of everyone at Courtwood Photographic Ltd., of Penzance cannot be underestimated – I owe then a great debt of gratitude. I would also like to thank Glenys Wass {Curator} and Peta Cook of Peterborough Museum for their help in allowing me use of my 1960's photographs of a 'city under change' which were lodged with the sadly missed Curator, Martin Howe, in 1985. Thanks must also go to Abacus Colour Printers for consent to reproduce the photograph of St. Anthony's Church, Cartmel Fell for which, they advise me, there is no known copyright assigned to a photographer. The photograph of the Peterborough Utd., 1960-61 squad also appears to have no copyright owner ; should anyone have knowledge of the copyright would they please contact the author. I herewith acknowledge that extensive attempts have been made to contact the photographer/author Colin Walker and his publisher Oxford Publishing Co., to seek permission to reproduce Plates 48 and 54 in his book 'Trails of Steam Vol. 2.

Trails through Peterborough but without success. These photographs are thus reproduced and the copyright of Colin Walker and Oxford Publishing Co., duly acknowledged. The extracts from John Clare's poetry are reproduced with the kind permission of The Curtis Brown Group Ltd., London on behalf of Eric Robinson.

I must also mention the 'four gentlemen' I met one boiling hot summer day by the Triangular Bridge in Crowland {see the Introduction}. They were a revelation and a pleasure to talk to. If I'd had more time they would no doubt have written my next book for me! Dick Bates, George Hammond, Harry Steels and Bernard Carr – long may you prosper! I have spoken and chatted with many others during my travels – they were unknown to me then and remain anonymous today. To them – many thanks.

I must mention the late Brian Redhead who sadly died in 1994 at such a young age. The author of 'Months in the Country', he was a brilliant journalist and broadcaster and wonderfully evocative writer. I recall with much pleasure his time on the Radio 4 'Today' programme. Brian and his irresistible book 'Months in the Country' were my inspiration to write about the countryside, villages, towns and cities and personalities I have had the pleasure of knowing since childhood. The Fen born author Edward Storey, whose many books capture the very feel and atmosphere of Fenland, the city of Peterborough and his home town of Whittlesey certainly influenced me and gave me inspiration.

Peterborough Utd., { The Posh } have been magnificent - Steve and Chris Brewer alongside Leigh

Porter and all the administration staff. My thanks to the club for releasing the copyright of two superb colour photographs which are reproduced with their kind permission. Also my sincere thanks for use of facilities at the club for the launch of this book. I must not forget the indefatigable Barry Fry – yes, Barry, I did buy your book 'Big Fry', and it's a great read!

The staff at the Carmarthen and Cardiff stores of Jessops Ltd., must also be mentioned. In particular Lisa Wride and Adrian Jones who have given support and advice concerning the Canon cameras and equipment that have been purchased from them. I should also mention the staff at BBC Radio Cambridgeshire for interviewing me on the Breakfast and Afternoon Shows about the launch of my book – many thanks.

Inestimable thanks must go to long time friends Sandra and Colin Langwade of Peterborough who have provided me with 5 Star hospitality and supported me through 'thick and thin'. When I felt defeated they persuaded me to push on and complete the book. Many thanks Colin for coming to the rescue at the last minute and providing me with photographs that I needed for inclusion in the book – you, of course, will be duly acknowledged!

Finally to my family who have put up with my often erratic, artistic temperament – their forbearance has been commendable.

CONTENTS

IV Time to travel

Seaside Sorcery
Spreading the word
Baby it's cold outside
Plastic fantastic
War and peace
Slow and dirty
Rockin' all over the world
At peace with the world
Call it a Tuscan Country
Heaven is 'Nowhere'

V Rural Matters

Ozone and all
Hairy Ned
Down the garden path
What rot!
Morgues and mowers
Endangered species
Badgers and barn owls
Nothing to do with us guv!
High and mighty
Gathering clouds
Now and forever

VI It's a mad mad world

Witches and warlocks
Superstitious chickens
Saints alive!
Glad tidings be upon you
Frying tonight
Will the last person in Wales
please turn out the light

ILLUSTRATIONS

Between pages 80 and 81

The Butter Cross and War Memorial, Market Square, Whittlesey

By Moreton's Leam in the Nene Washes, Eldernell

The Five Chimneys latterly the White Swan pub at Sea Level, Tick Fen, Warboys

The Baptist Chapel, Warboys

Old brick bridge, dated 1833, over Thorney River, Murrow

Browne's Hospital, Stamford

Derelict Tudor Farm, Earning Street, Godmanchester

Restored and lived in Tudor Farm, Earning Street, Godmanchester

The West Front, Crowland Abbey

The Triangular Bridge, Crowland

Old cottage by Thorney River, Thorney

Fen subsidence – Gothic House Farm, French Drove, North Fen amidst flax

Distant view of Stamford and it's churches from the west

The Clare Memorial, Helpston

Helpston Church and John Clare's grave

SoutheyWood, near Helpston in Clare Country

St Vincent's Cross, Nene Terrace, looking to Singlesole and Morris Fen

Thorney River, Murrow, looking towards Parson Drove

The donkeys with owner David Smith on the beach by the Grand Pier, Weston super Mare

Looking towards the former Knightstone Theatre and Baths, Weston super Mare

The Grand Pier, Weston super Mare

The donkeys by the Grand Pier, Weston super Mare

Woodwalton Church, far from it's village, on a hillock above the Fens

The church of St Egwad, Llanfynydd

Cartmel Fell Church, Lake District

A Class 4F prepares to leave Peterborough East under the elevated signalbox

The crowd cheering victorious Posh at the Division 2 Play Off Final at Wembley, May 2000

Eldest son, Chris, celebrating at the Wembley victory, May 2000

Recent action of the Posh { blue kit }, London Road Stadium, Peterborough Utd FC

The South Stand, London Road Stadium, Peterborough Utd FC

'Nowhere' amidst the lilies, Old Town, St Mary's, Isles of Scilly

The cottage garden through the wicket gate at 'Nowhere', Old Town, St Mary's, Isles of Scilly

Old Town Church from the footpath alongside Old Town Bay, St Mary's, Isles of Scilly

The Greenwich Meridian sign alongside the Old Nene, Flood's Ferry

St Martin's looking across to Tresco, Isles of Scilly

Monmouthshire and Brecon Canal near Talybont on Usk

Coed Clathen Battlefield, Broad Oak, Carms.

Trichrug, Carn Goch and Towy Valley from near Defadfa Isaf

The Mad Cat public house at Pidley near Warboys

Carew Castle, Pembs. across tidal creek

Carreg Cennen Castle, The Black Mountain, Carms.

Cadge and Colman's Flour Mill {now demolished} beside the River Nene, Peterborough

Photographic acknowledgements

The author wishes to thank those who have kindly given their permission to reproduce the following photographs :

Abacus Colour Printers
     - Cartmel Fell Church

Colin Walker & Oxford Publishing Co.
     - A Class V2 heads for Kings Cross above the Fair Meadow, Peterborough
     - A Class 4F prepares to leave Peterborough East under the signalbox

Graham Mealand
     - Biographical photograph of the author taken on the Isles of Scilly

Peterborough Museum
     - St John's Church and White Horse, Peterborough

- Deacon's School & Perkins Factory, Deacon Street, Peterborough
- Waterloo Arcade, Peterborough
- Sweet Briar Walk, Peterborough

Peterborough Utd FC {the posh.com}
- The South Stand, London Road Stadium, Peterborough
- Recent action shot of the Posh at London Road Stadium

Colin Langwade
- The 8 lane A1{M} at Norman Cross, Peterborough

Island Sea Safaris {Mark & Susie Groves}
- Two photographs of the cottage garden at 'Nowhere', Old Town, St Mary's, Isles of Scilly

INTRODUCTION

'Why you'm writin' about fens an' mountains?' asked one of the rugged, weatherbeaten old men sitting in front of the triangular bridge in Crowland.

'If you'm a fenman as you sez then surely you sticks to the fens - them mountains are jus' forin' parts!'

He had a point.

The day was hot - no - excessively hot and my ice cream from the village shop across the road was melting faster than I could consume it. But it didn't concern the four old gentlemen watching the world go by. I was just about to comment on the heat and my childhood summers when one of them suddenly spoke again.

'You'm gone thro' a fen winter?'

'Yes' I replied 'The winter of 1947 - the hardest in recent times'.

For the first time they looked stunned and seemed to accept they were truly speaking to one of their own.

I don't really wish to recall being born during one of the worst winters in living memory but rather remember those innocent childhood summers that are too vivid to forget. Memories mature just like a fine wine. Maybe we need to be exiled so that we can come to terms with where we truly belong and fully appreciate the untold joys we experienced in the fields and meadows where we used to play. To return to a place which we have held with some affection can be disastrous and we may well be angry and disenchanted with what we find. We change as well as time and places! Many would accuse me of looking through rose tinted spectacles at a past, which, if I were honest, would be a massive shock if we were transported back in time. But the past is the past - it is just enjoyable to allow the memory to lapse into a state of oblivion and wallow in making these childhood days what we wish.

'Where you'm from now?'

'West Wales - East Carmarthenshire to be precise. But I've travelled all over Britain and abroad'.

Fenman can be stubborn, kind, dull and humorous but they are wonderful listeners and amazing talkers - at their own pace! True to form a couple of the gentlemen started discussing how they became involved with a Welsh Regiment in the war and how some of the Welshmen decided to take up farming - a subject close to their hearts in the fens. As the old gentlemen were only too aware the fens can often seem to be mile upon mile of unending fields. But the fens and vast swathes of the country are more than just fields, woods, moor land and mountain. It is impossible to pass by the heritage and history of Bath, Cirencester and Stamford, the seaside sorcery of Weston super Mare the stunning scenery of Wales, the Lakes and the Isles of Scilly and even the timeless tranquillity of the Tuscan countryside must rank amidst the best there is to be seen. They all deserve a mention - all have scenes to be set and tales to be told. You cannot travel this country without remembering Hereward the Wake, Oliver Cromwell, John Clare, Daniel Lambert, Vermuyden, Wordsworth and Shelley, Mary Queen of Scots and Katherine of Aragon and so many others.

'This book then - what's it about then?' one of the old gentlemen enquired, not expecting the answer that came back.

'The past, the present and the future - about events, people and places - in fact everything that makes this land such a rich tapestry'.

They appeared totally bemused.

'It's good to leave your birthplace and see the sights and sounds of your own country and those abroad'. The old men were numbed into silence. 'But you can always return to appreciate your "home" and reflect upon the wider world'.

One of the gentlemen eyed me suspiciously up and down before making a most profound statement in a lugubrious fen drawl.

'You'm roigt about that'

Our country is changing so rapidly that many of us feel helpless and disorientated - old buildings are swept away, field after field fall victim to a sprawling housing estate or some impersonal supermarket, once loved footpaths and byways are lost and dual carriageways and motorways spring out of nothing. Some of the changes wreck the landscape beyond recognition and we are all guilty of indifference to the reality and impact that climate change will have on our whole way of life. Thankfully some things resist change or are just fortunate to escape - these landscapes, scenes and village or town environments retain their distinct 'spirit of place'. They are becoming few and far between but hopefully they will survive along with festivals and age - old traditions that have served their inhabitants well for many centuries.

Few places can be judged on a fleeting glimpse, a weekend or even over a season. On one of my recent forays into the Cambridgeshire fens I decided it was well worth the risk of taking a narrow road, or rather track, that had no signpost at all. I should have ended my journey at Turves still deep in the fens but the road finished abruptly after some 300 yards at a rickety old bridge spanning the confluence of the Old River Nene and the Whittlesey Dike. Floods Ferry as it is known was no more and I was marooned on the bank of the river. My disappointment turned to enjoyment - the scene of a placid river, as calm as a millpond, drifting lazily in the warm summer sunshine against a background of reed beds and luscious verdant trees was just so idyllic - it reminded me of the scenes that were set in the novel Wind in the Willows with characters such as Ratty, Mole and Badger. I remained lost in its beauty. This is certainly one place I shall be returning to time and time again to sample its special ambiance.

I would recommend you allow yourself time to become absorbed in the very atmosphere of a place, whether it be in the Fens, the Lakes or the Cotswolds. Try not to hurry as you may miss a stunning sunset or the mist lifting at dawn across an ethereal landscape. Grasp the moment while you can. Remember that the climate in this small island of ours is changing dramatically; what we see now will change beyond recognition in the next 50 years. The fen landscape, in particular, is in the very throes of concluding it's impressive history and will once more return to the sea from whence it came. Savour its glory now for it will never be the same again - man has seen to that!

I apologise for ending on such a sombre note but I trust you will enjoy the reminiscences, impressions and thought provoking views of my travels from fen to mountain.

KM
Llanfynydd 2004

I

FOREVER HOME

FOREVER HOME

Truthfully I remember little of the house where I was first brought up in our home village in the Fens save to say that we had wide open fields behind the garden which in deepest summer were rich with golden corn and the swaying heads of pillar box poppies. Summers then seemed so hot and summery and winters so cold and wintry. My sister, 3 years my elder ,probably had further reason to remember our first home - it was she, I recall ,who sat on a bee on the garden shed doorstep with painful consequences and also lost her shoes for good in a very muddy field when returning home from the village school the wrong way. No doubt some avid local archaeologist will unearth her shoes in years to come.

Apart from the occasional visit to the small market town nearby which I distinctly remember sported a rather fine and individualistic market clock on a leaf bedecked cast iron column, village life inexorably revolved around the family, farming, school and the chapel - much as it had done for generations before. Other than some infrequent high jinks at throwing out time from the locals, a much - prized scalp in a village football match which was inevitably celebrated for an inordinate time and the passage of the battered green and cream United Counties market day bus, life was peaceful and unruffled

For some years following our move to the nearby city of Peterborough the family regularly visited my grandparents home at the centre of the old village. The journey by bus across the inhospitable Fens was fascinating for us as children but certainly no picnic for out parents. Fate had dictated that the red and cream City bus stopped some 8 miles short of the village. If luck was on your side the green and cream Country bus met you under the market clock to take you at a leisurely pace onto your destination. But it didn't always work out that way. Seemingly hours could be spent consulting timetables by means of a flickering streetlight in freezing temperatures and with snow falling to blot out all sounds apart from the thumping together of numbed hands. Was this really Cambridgeshire or could it have been Siberia ?

Weekend visits and in particular Christmas festivities at what was once a pub, aptly named the Prince of Wales' Feathers, were the highlight of the year. The old building oozed history from every nook and cranny - the cool haunting cellar, the homely kitchen with the black iron range and rows of meat hooks set in serried ranks across the ceiling and the brightly coloured oilcloth covering a massive table furnished with a mouth watering display of every conceivable delicacy. The old parlour was just as welcoming. An enormous long table covered by a burgundy red velvet tasselled tablecloth and crisp white damask sheet lay prepared for high tea. Sitting on the old mantelshelf were a set of ancient brass candlesticks and a shell case from the First World War now acting as a general odds and ends pot whilst by the fire stood a weather beaten easy chair that had seen generations of use.

Somehow after stuffing ourselves with cold meats and pies, pickles, salads and buttered bread followed by every imaginable cake, ice cream fruit and fizzy drink, we were cajoled and squeezed into our Sunday best for the short walk to evening service at the Methodist Chapel across the road. I have often wondered whether our family were noted in Chapel for the sundry gastronomic noises that could be heard rising and falling above the preachers dialogue; I just assumed at the time that my fidgeting was purely down to a childish desire to shed the shackles of suit and tie and be free to explore the old house. Attendance at evening services was obligatory save you suffered some life threatening illness but I would have given anything to be anywhere but in Chapel; pinned down to a straight backed and excruciatingly hard pew whilst suffering the torture of some dreary sermon offered little solace to a young boy. Oh how I wish I'd had the acumen of my father and his friends when, as young lads, they were not averse to 'working the market' in pursuance of some monetary gain. Regularly they stood under the village clock tower early every Saturday morning to waylay the organist on his way to practice at the parish church - if the organist was obliging they received the princely sum of 6 pence for operating the organ bellows! I never did find out if all of the lads pumped the organ and shared the 6 pence or one was selected to be the 'chosen one' and went home very happy!

Sadly in the 60's the old house was pulled about and swept away like so many others at that time in a tide of 'modernisation', which left the old pub with no character or heart. In recent years I have frequently passed the house on the way up the village street towards the Clock Tower and the Weir but it's just not the same. The Chapel is still there and very much as I knew it but alas the White Hart pub next door is gone, victim of a vicious fire.

Strangely I still vividly remember one particular aspect of those incredible gargantuan teas - the upright glass vase containing sticks of crisp fenland celery! Memories are still strong.

Footnote : The White Hart has been rebuilt to it's former glory so that incongruous juxtaposition of pub and abstaining Methodists once more stand side by side in the village street!

II

EARLY
MEMORIES

FEASTS AND FUNDAYS

It must be at least 35 years since I enjoyed a ride on the dodgems!

Feasts and fairs were once the 'red letter' event in every village and small town across the country and had been so since time immemorial when they were the only available entertainment for many rural folk. Moat inhabitants had never ventured further than their own small insular community relying totally on 'travelling shows' for some fun and light relief from the monotony and drudgery of a harsh life. Some villages and towns still host similar events but on nothing like the scale of days gone by. Most are but remnants of their former glory - a reminder of royal patronage to a market or fair worked carefully around the farming calendar and the Saints Days. Markets, travelling theatre and fairground attractions along with side stalls offered country folk from far and wide the chance to 'let their hair down' and enjoy themselves. Frequently many of the visitors would not be seen again for another year when once more they would put their glad rags on and make the journey to their few long awaited days of fun, feasting and spending.

One of the ways in which I remember the annual feast in our Fenland village was strangely the re routing of the green and cream United Counties omnibus around some of the virtually unknown lanes - backwaters that I had never ventured down - in order to avoid the feast that had been set up in the main street. I can remember gazing in admiration at the stands and large lorries with generators lined up in the High Street, some almost touching the window sills of the houses, as we rejoined the normal route further down the village. Even the Jubilee Clock, normally resplendent at the triangle of roads that met at it's base, was surrounded by every conceivable machine and stall and only just managed to remind people of it's presence. I suppose one consolation was that the clock face could still be seen - as long as you stood far enough back! A haze of exhaust smoke from the generators hung in the air and filtered across the many coloured lights that hung from stands and rides but which dimmed and brightened as if in unison with the rise and fall of the great machines as they struggled to cope with the load. I couldn't wait to alight from the bus close to my grandparent's house and run back up the street and seek out the dodgems, of course! By the time I was in my early teens the feast was already on the downward path and not a patch on what it had been some 30 years earlier when my father had enjoyed the thrills and spills of the feast and fair as a lad.

I am told it always took place in July during the week following the Big Fair in the local market town of Ramsey and on Feast Day, as it was known, the heavy equipment dragged itself the 5 or 6 miles into the village. The huge long trailers, stacked high with the 'bits' that made up stalls and rides, were hauled by magnificent steam traction engines sporting the name Henry Thurston in gold letters on the roof canopy and displaying highly polished brass work over the whole machine. To set the feast off in the accustomed manner the Rectory gardens were opened to the public on the Sunday with entertainment provided by one or more of the local brass bands - no doubt complimented by the ubiquitous cup of tea and cucumber sandwiches served by the Church ladies! The Tuesday night at the feast was always the most popular as the fen workers poured into the village to spend their hard earned money - money that had accumulated to considerable sums by the end of the vegetable growing season and was paid out by agreement with their employers at the mid point of the feast when they enjoyed their only 'holiday'. My father often recalled the roundabout entitled 'Jollity Farm' and the dodgems which the young lads of the village always made a mad dash for. The dodgem rides which cost 6d never ever lasted long enough and quite frequently, he tells me they tried, as there was unofficially room for two in the cars, to stay for 3 consecutive sessions as long as they had enough 'tanners' to pay. As the dodgems were so popular it became quite an art to grab a car almost before it's occupants had had time to get out!

Whatever the weather the village stores, and in particular the Fish and Chip shop, did well. Mr Bradley and his wife somehow coped with the incessant demand for their wonderful fare - 2d for a piece of cod and a 1d for a bag of chips made of course from best Fen potatoes - what else? When my father started work in the late 30's just before the war he earned the princely sum of 15 shillings a week and always, as a matter of course, had a fish and chip supper on Saturdays and ¾ lb of chocolate toffee for the weekend. How times have changed! Cod is even an endangered species now, just some 60 years on.

At the opposite end of the calendar around Plough Sunday was the Straw Bear Festival. Steeped in tradition, folklore and superstition it is nothing like the village feast but rather a good excuse to join in the fun and indulge in an extended pub crawl! It was not until we became proud owners of our little thatched cottage in the fenland market town of Whittlesey that we came into contact with this strange and some would say bizarre festival. It had taken a young Geordie many years to investigate and unearth the background of this once very important festival which had fallen into disuse, like so many others, and resurrect a bonanza of dance, street theatre and of course booze. Based on superstition and tradition that could be traced into medieval times it brought to life for country folk, many of whom must have been illiterate, the need for fertility and successful crops at the start of what was seen as the new year. The centrepiece was then, and still is a man dressed in a sheaf of straw - the Straw Bear - paraded through the streets on a length of rope by a 'fool' and accompanied by sword dancers, fire eaters, molly men, morris and clog dancers. It couldn't have been that difficult then as now for the poor unfortunate, or maybe fortunate, soul in the straw to break for a rest and a jar or two at a pub around the town. Miraculously the distance between each ale house appeared to reduce as the 'tour' reached it's conclusion - hardly surprising that the Straw Bear was totally inebriated by the end of his duties! Possibly the only dignified part of the festival came on Plough Sunday when all were summoned to service at the Parish Church but I doubt if the 'bear' or many of his supporters were in a fit state to take part.

Few of the many feasts, fairs and festivals survived the 2nd World War although some like the Straw Bear carry on in something like their original form. Events such as the Furry Dance, Wassailing the Apple Tree, Punky Night and Clipping the Church are still celebrated as part of the religious and farming calendar depicting the struggle between good and evil, light and darkness and of course the fertile spring and the sterile winter. Other fairs and festivals are less obvious in their continued celebrations, no doubt the true reasons being lost in the mists of time - Widecombe Fair and Uncle Tom Cobleigh, the Stilton Cheese Rolling and a host of Pancake Races, Midsummer, Gooseberry, Sheep, Horse and Bridge Fairs. The Mummers Plays and Street Theatre are no longer needed except as a possible tourist spectacle now that education has spread across the whole of society.

As winter fast approaches my mind turns to the farmers ploughing in the stubble with their team of heavy horses and preparing the land for the next crop. Horse drawn ploughs may be a thing of the past but we certainly still need to 'plough the fields and scatter the good seed on the ground'. Pity the poor villagers where the Plough Play is still re - enacted - if you didn't feel inclined to join in the fun and merriment and offer gifts or money to the 'plough jacks' as the decorated plough stopped outside your house then your front garden stood a good chance of being ploughed up!

Blessed be the plough and long live our feasts and festivals.

Footnote : I recently visited the Warboys Feast with my youngest son and rode on the dodgems!!!!!

CELERY, CARROTS AND COAL

Being raised in the vast open spaces of the fen countryside, where biting easterly winds tore at your very soul as soon as you put a foot out of the door, was not a good introduction to the ways of British Rail.

By the time I had rather unwillingly entered the village primary school many of the rural lines criss crossing the fields had already gone before even our 'dear friend' Doctor Beeching could further lay waste the system. Small unsung stations and halts with evocative yet strange sounding names such as Black Bank, Shippea Hill, Smeeth Road and Six Mile Bottom were consigned along with their characters, lifelike and legendary, to the history books. Occasionally I still come across them whilst browsing the shelves in some small fascinating bookshop hidden away from mainstream shopping.

Despite living in the middle of nowhere our village was served by a line that had its terminus - probably too grand a term - at the nearby market town of Ramsey. The line then meandered and wandered through vast unending fields by an ingeniously circuitous route to the towns of Somersham and St. Ives and finally Cambridge. By some quirk of fate or possibly design, I'm not sure which, Ramsey possessed not one but two termini to serve the 2000 souls - they were aptly named the South and North stations! The line from the North station was laid across some of the richest agricultural land which produced the highest quality celery, carrots, sugar beet and potatoes. As if in fear of despoiling this wonderful soil it's route appeared to be more akin to a Roman Road with hardly a curve in the alignment until it reached the East Coast mainline where it's branch engines met their big brothers at Holme.

I must digress, however, and take you on a short detour to Holme Fen Nature Reserve and Whittlesey Mere where you can experience the very essence and qualities of Fen landscape – endless and limitless skies with horizons far, far away, crystal clear light and mirror bright water in dykes and lakes. Sedges and reeds lining dykes sway gently in the light wind whilst the recent wet weather makes the dramatic jet black peat soil bounce under your feet. The Reserve, now part of the Great Fen Project, is a paradise of wildfowl, marsh plants, mosses, ferns and the largest area in the country of pure birch woodland.

The arrow straight track through the Reserve alongside Holme Lode is deserted despite there being close by one of the most important Fenland monuments – the Holme Fen Posts – displaying the alarming rate at which the Fen peat land is being lost. The first cast iron post of some 12 feet in length, driven into the peat in 1851 came from the Great Exhibition but had to be supplemented by a second post in 1963 so that the monitoring of peat shrinkage could continue. The Great Exhibition Post almost fell over and needed support as 12 feet of peat had been lost in just over 100 years! If you visit the posts today and the lost soil were to be restored you would be 20 feet below what the ground level had once been or 8 feet below sea level!!!!!!!! The Reserve holds the dubious title of being the lowest point in Britain – what a sobering thought!!!

Just a stone's throw away from the Posts along the trackway by Holme Lode is the site of Whittlesey Mere – the last stretch of inland water, the size of Derwent Water in the Lakes, to be drained from the Fens in the 19th. Century. You can stand on the track by Holme Lode and look across the flat landscape of some 3000 acres that was once the Mere. In its hay day it was a haven of wildfowl, rare butterflies and moths and a host of all types of fish and eels. The Mere hosted many regattas and shows that attracted hoards of local people and visitors and must have been a sight to behold. Even John Clare, the poet, walked from his home village of Helpston, north of Peterborough, to the Mere to study the rare ferns and plants and immerse himself in the atmosphere and peacefulness. The loss of the 2000 year old Mere was lamented by many – boatmen, naturalists and fishermen. If we could turn the clock back it would have been far better if it had been kept. The sudden drainage of 3000 acres had an enormous impact on peat shrinkage probably pushing the Holme Fen Post 2 feet out of the ground!!!!!!!! What a joy the Mere would have been for us today – or would it have succumbed to the all too familiar speedboats and water skiing along with their attendant fast food outlets? Probably it was best that it was drained! It is now just silent, pancake flat fields with their ripening crops stretching as far as the eye can see.

There is intimate silence in the woodland. In the surrounding fen fields the silence is overpowering.

This is true Fen.

Returning, which I must, to the Celery, Carrots and Coal line, a minimal passenger service existed on both lines out of Ramsey until losses could no longer be sustained only to be outlived by occasional excursion trains from the southern terminus. These were laid on to take willing and eager youngsters and their reluctant guardians on the long 'mystery' tour to the seaside at Hunstanton. For some time after all vestiges of a passenger service had been lost an irregular freight train plied up and down from the North terminus doing yeoman service ahead of the time when most farmers decided it was better to own or at least hire lorries to take their produce to regional or London markets.

There was one thing I was sure of by the time I left the Fens for city life and that was the quality of the celery, carrots and potatoes. It is well known that many a Fen farmer became rich beyond the wildest dreams of us all on the proceeds of these three humble vegetables. Even after we had left the Fens I couldn't escape these vegetables! The cycle trips through the Fens either to spend time at my grandparent's house or to collect our annual supply of plums and apples from Uncle George brought me constantly into contact with them. It was as certain as night follows day that we would pass field upon field of vegetables in the process of being harvested and loaded onto waiting tractor drawn trailers, creaking ominously on their axles in the jet black soil, and battered old lorries which had definitely seen better days. More often than not we would have little choice but take evasive action to avoid heaps of soil and vegetables that had fallen onto the highway from the groaning transport taking their loads to the railway terminus. Celery was rarely encountered as this was normally packed along with its cloak of black soil into strong wooden crates. Sugar beet were a prized possession particularly near Halloween when they were hollowed out complete with grotesque faces to receive candles for the celebrations

As so often happened when we approached Ramsey we were greeted by the toot of whistle and the hiss of the branch line steam engine as it clanked it's way into the terminus resplendent with it's lightweight train of two wagons and a smoking guards van. By the time we reached the terminus the little train had finished it's journey and was busily and happily shunting the wagons into the correct order for the imminent return to the mainline at Holme. One wagon, I remember, was almost reverently shunted to a bay platform where a battered old lorry stood patiently waiting to collect it's load - not vegetables but coal - sufficient to keep the town and surrounding villages in fuel for another week or more. As if by magic tractors and lorries arrived laden with the fat of the land - celery, carrots, potatoes and sugar beet, all to be loaded into the waiting wagons. Not until tractors and lorries became more common place did this scenario take place but rather the farmers relied on leaving their goods at small wooden loading platforms alongside the railway line where the driver and fireman would halt the train for farmhands to manhandle the goods into the trucks. One wonders how on earth the driver and the fireman knew who had loaded what goods onto the train and who had taken delivery en route! It was a truly 'door to door' community service where presumably each and everyone knew everybody else! Regrettably it has all vanished.

My fascination with this diminutive but most important little branch line haunts me. I can still remember the grimy old tank engine, usually a J6 from Peterborough's massive New England Depot and which hadn't seen a clean in many a long year but still managed to give yeoman service. It gently simmered in the platform, occasionally letting out a sudden hiss of steam as if in anticipation and impatience to be on the way. The railway line is all but gone now although the track bed is still traceable in places as it cuts it's way straight as an arrow across the fen fields. There are still small remnants of the North station terminus and until some 10 years ago parts of the platform defiantly denied the invading weeds. All are but a distant memory of happier days.

This was the closest I ever came to British Rail in the Fens and what I saw I liked immensely - far better than the brash and furious mainlines. It was personal and community led - homely and very special.

Let's have more celery, carrots and coal!

GOOD OLD UNCLE GEORGE

I can remember with great affection and delight the glorious and contented days of high summer when lazily wandering through the tall waving grass of an orchard rich with plums, damsons and gages dripping from the trees. Unlike the seasonal workers my Uncle George had hired for picking I was able to proudly walk with complete authority though constantly having to remind myself that there was a job to be done despite the glorious sunshine.

My uncle had made what proved to be an important and shrewd decision after leaving the army at the end of the 2nd.World War - there were rich pickings in the fruit growing industry around Bluntisham, Colne and Earith in the Huntingdonshire Fens. As a young lad I would think nothing of cycling alongside my father the 16 miles to my home village and grandparents house and once duly fortified trace the remaining 7 miles or so over hillier terrain to Uncle George's orchard on the edge of the Fens. It didn't seem to matter in those heady days of the late 50's and early 60's whether we were caught on the open road in an August thunderstorm and arrived at our destination looking more akin to drowned (and steaming } rats than avid cyclists out to enjoy the rural scenery. Mad as it may seem today, the aim was to return to Peterborough with a stone of 'vic' plums – few I'm sure today would put themselves through this 'torture'. This annual ritual was maintained at least until I became the proud possessor of my first car - a Triumph Herald - upon which event the family succumbed to using the internal combustion engine to obtain our supply of plums. Somehow the fascination of the 'plum run' was lost once the bicycle was sidelined to the garden shed never to be dusted down, oiled up and prepared for it's journey into fruit growing territory.

We had always regarded the 'outward' run to be 'light' and it was almost as if the cycles knew the route without us having to guide, them unless of course we stopped off to have a few words with my Great Aunt Lil Christmas at the big thatched farmhouse in Wood End in Bluntisham. There is little I can recall of Great Aunt save to say I was awestruck when presented to an imposing white haired old lady sitting majestically in a large armchair amidst the gloom of the badly lit parlour. Behind her would have been an enormous inglenook fireplace complete with it's ancient dog irons and the remains of the previous night's fire. Both house and aunt emitted a 'presence' of history and a nagging feeling that those who had lived and died within its walls were still present and watching! It was not until quite recently that we learnt that my aunt's family had been Quakers and many were buried at the Meeting House in the High Street just round the corner. Before I left I was always given a bronze three penny piece; in spite of the financial gain I was always pleased to be 'released' into the bright sunshine and fresh air of the August day once, of course, I had said my polite thanks and goodbyes. My father often talked of Great Aunt Lil, the Manor Farm and the Christmas family. As a lad he was offered three pence to look after the bullocks in the yard but I have never truly discovered whether this was regarded as a 'chore' worth doing for financial gain or was a job to be avoided at all costs. He and his elder brother, still of Junior School age, often spent a weeks holiday in the summer helping their Aunt Lil and Uncle Leonard. He was amazed that they did not appear to lose any animals on the frequent 2 mile drive down the lanes to new pasture or guide them into the wrong field. As the beasts shot off down the village street like a bullet out of a gun neither of them had little or no control; if they reached the right field my father was convinced it was more by luck than judgement although it was quite conceivable they knew their own way! Thankfully they never met any cars or lorries on the highway. The Christmas family still own Manor Farm but the Quaker way of life has, I imagine, long ceased to be important. To this day the old Quaker Meeting House and its burial ground still stands testament to the faith in the High Street a reminder of how village life used to be - no doubt it could tell a tale or two.

It was always a relief to reach Uncle George's orchards so that we could rest a while ahead of the pleasure of plum picking. The picking season was a true community affair not unlike the harvesting of the wheat and hay. Although the orchards were not in the heart of the village his 'pickers' were the same every year - local Romanies in their brightly painted caravans with rope washing lines and battered billycans. Parents, grandparents, children, grandchildren, aunts and uncles all came to help in the harvest of the fruits and Uncle George and Aunty Peggy knew each and every one by name. George and Peggy practised something akin to transhumance, the age old practice of walking stock from summer to winter pastures and seen until the early years of the 20th.century in many parts of Wales. In their case it wasn't stock but human movement - themselves! During the picking season they left their house in the village and transferred their belongings to the weighing and packing station at the orchards where they would live on site until all fruit had been collected, weighed, packed and sent to market. I am told they had all the creature comforts they needed to keep them going the long hours they had to work.

Despite the hard backbreaking work we always enjoyed a wonderful welcome from my uncle who had I'm sure become used to seeing us with the 'peck' potato basket ready for action. Suitable niceties over we were despatched down one side of the orchard away from the main pickers, tractors and trailers. There always seemed to be hoards of pickers swarming over the trees in every direction and loading basketfuls of fruit onto trailers ready to be trundled back down the rows to the packing and weighing station. Box upon box along with it's attendant wasps stood like sentries outside and inside the station with brightly marked labels advising of their impending destination - Covent Garden, Liverpool, Manchester or just the local markets. I so wished it could have happened every week throughout the year so good was the fruit – that was until, of course, you put your hand on a wasp! Two or three hours later with basket full and the heady aroma of plums still wafting around us we paid Uncle George the princely sum of sixpence a pound and staggered from the orchard gate with the loaded basket balanced on the handlebars of my father's bike. With the great temptation of the plums in the basket we retraced our way back, this time at a far slower pace, to my home village for a short 'layover'. Leaving behind some of our prize haul of plums (which always saddened me) and some 'cookers' we resumed our weary track across the pancake flat land of the Fens to reach home just as the sun was setting like a deep crimson ball in the western sky.

Uncle George didn't make a fortune like so many at that time but enough to live off comfortably. When the orchards were sold off it must have felt as if part of his body had been wrenched from him as it had been so much part of his life. The orchards may well have changed hands many times since and one in particular next to the former Chatteris - St. Ives railway line - strangely the very one we always visited - has had the fruit trees grubbed up like so many others around the country. The loss is much more than a production process for apples and plums, rather more a way of life within a once close - knit community. I wonder where the Romany families that once helped my uncle have gone? The glorious spectacle of spring fruit blossom has all disappeared along with the wildlife and those infernal wasps. But we don't seem to care or even notice. Sad to say it is a sign of the ever - advancing European market economy and avaricious businessmen intent on squeezing every penny available from their assets whatever the effect on our countryside. The loss of my uncle's orchards and many others across the country carries an enormous penalty - a loss to the British palate. The good old English apples, plums, pears and damsons for some strange reason just do not meet the 'European' standard and the new expectations of the housewife - perfectly shaped, unblemished and reliably standard in size, squeaky clean and tasteless! We mark the passing of such famous and evocative sounding fruits as Egremont Russet, Millers Seedling, Tydemans Early, Morgan Sweet and Tom Putt, Monarch President and Severn Cross but then lay out the red carpet for Golden and Red Delicious - wonderful sounding names but certainly not in the mould of the British apple and plum.

Looking back it seems my uncle was something of a pioneering spirit as well as being champion of the true community life now so lacking in our towns and villages - the pressure of the newly acclaimed global economy with it's attendant supermarket invasion and fickle housewives finally sealed the fate of his business. It may well be the same orchards are now host to some crop for which the EEC hands out exorbitant sums with little or no regard to the excessive production which will find itself stored away in some distant warehouse despite the ongoing 3rd.world famine. The thought that housing may have invaded this almost sacred land does not even bear consideration – I just could not contemplate it. It's a mad, mad world.

All these years later it still amazes me how so much of the fruit in that basket ever reached home for bottling in kilner jars, stewing for pies or eating cold on a boiling hot summer day - no freezers in those days, at least not in our household.

Long live the Vic plum - good old Uncle George!

DOWN MEMORY LANE

Little do you realise at the tender age of sixteen that what you pass and see everyday of your life is but transient and will one day disappear or at least be changed beyond recognition only to be replaced by a modern day vernacular.

Somehow I cannot see today's buildings designed for the lifespan of a man lasting and being revered as of special architectural merit and warranting their protection for future generations to admire. There really can be no more vernacular building in the truest sense of the word than that era of traditional buildings typified by the use of local materials and skills, faithfully honouring their own peculiar 'dialect'.

I recall little of the cathedral city to which our family moved when I was just five save that I have no difficulty in remembering the primary school I attended. A tall, grim Late Victorian Board School, it stood proudly, as if a reminder of the foreboding school regime, on possibly the only eminence in the city apart that is from the rise that was crowned by the Cathedral. I vividly remember the bell high in it's turret at the very top of the building but strangely can never remember it being rung for start of school. How could anyone forget the draughty inhospitable outside toilets, the fanciful iron playground railings which hinted at keeping children in as well as preventing the 'unwanted' entering and the high glazed partitions which separated classrooms from a lofty central assembly hall where the headmistress 'held court' each morning. At the back of the hall were those poor stuffed birds and animals gathering dust in cavernous glass cases - it seemed that everywhere you travelled in the building the beady eyes of the owl(god rest it's soul) followed you. That sickly green or blue paint which must have been a 'standard' school colour met your gaze at every corner. Other memories are scant possibly on account of the urgent desire to leave school and return home to play with friends in the street - primary school was not a happy time.

Across the road from the school by the railway line stood a fascinating building decorated in terracotta panels with a green illuminated Colemans sign which glowed almost unnaturally at night; alongside it a bright red sign informed everyone Peterborough was just 1 mile - a beacon to all travellers arriving from London. This, as I was to discover later, was one of the original Colemans mustard factories and the blue and yellow barrels that adorned the front of the building in serried ranks contained nothing less than mustard and honey! The latter it appears was the ingredient for the famous Gales Honey which took pride of place in those days on every shelf of every shop in the land. The old factory survived in several guises including the processing and canning of peas until the building and the site inevitably succumbed to rationalisation and a favourite and cherished landmark was gone forever.

As I advanced to Deacons Grammar School my interest in the built heritage blossomed as I cycled each day through the historic heart of the city. Quite frequently after finishing a rugby match or muddy cross country I would call at the imposing and grand Town

Hall to meet up with my father before cycling home together for tea. Like so many Town Halls across the country this was no exception. Built to the glory of the Corporation it was adorned with vast sweeping marble staircases, plush velvet curtains hanging from immensely deep windows, elaborately decorated ceilings with glittering chandeliers and highly polished wood floors in which you could almost see your face. As young children my sister and I always looked forward to the Christmas party organised and paid for by the Corporation and held in the impressive Reception Room - a tall, vast and stately room which would have done credit to the Royal Family. Naturally I recall the 'fare' that met our eyes - jelly, ice cream, cakes and every conceivable delicacy - and the Christmas Tree, covered in lights of every colour, which reached to the very top of the room almost level with a curtained balcony from which Father Christmas made his entry. Strangely I still cannot remember how he descended to the floor with his bulging sack full of presents!

My cycle journeys through the city were pretty uneventful apart from the time I mowed down an elderly lady who had inadvertently strayed into the street opposite the tower doorway of St. John's Parish Church. Maybe I was asking too much of 'my machine' in an effort to get home for tea or possibly I was trying in vain not to be late for choir practice. The elderly lady survived the impact but my bike suffered considerable damage forcing me to walk it to its final destination! Our Grammar School was one of only two for boys the other being the Kings School - deadly rivals in everyway. The 'derby' rugby match for the 1st.XV's was not for the fainthearted and inevitably degenerated into a bloodbath with a master on hand ready to transport the 'wounded' to the local casualty department. The rival school also happened to be the Cathedral School providing choristers for the Bishop whilst we were left the crumbs - choristers at the Parish Church, not that this was without it's worthwhile perks. As time approached for Founders Day, Commemoration Services and the Festival of Nine Lessons and Carols the choristers were given special treatment with time off lessons and homework in order to practice under the watchful eye of the music master who we were reliably informed had been a personal friend of Sir Malcolm Sargent.

During my first year in grammar we were blessed with two sites between which we regularly plied much to our enjoyment, but certainly not to the masters. It did not last long and soon we were relocated to a new site north of the city centre at Queens Gardens. Anything must have been an improvement on the old buildings we vacated in what had been Crown Lane but was known to us as Deacons Street. Cramped, dirty, uneconomic and definitely not conducive to learning the old school stood immediately opposite the Perkins diesel engine testing plant which not only let out a constant roar and hum day and night but also spewed forth a cocktail of filthy fumes and steam into the sky. Even those '20 poor boys' in 1721 who were given the opportunity to 'read, write and cast accounts' whilst dressed in 'cinnamon suits with grey stockings' could not have suffered this affliction. One thing I can be sure of is that my initials and date were carved as so many others into the soft red brick of the chemistry lab wall for posterity - or so we thought! Sadly it has all gone - demolished to make way for the multi million pound Queensgate regional shopping centre redevelopment as part of a master plan for a New Town. All that is there to remind me is a simple plaque affixed to a column next to British Home Stores recording the site of my old school. Most rushing about their shopping and business in air - conditioned comfort do not even notice. It makes me wonder if that 'bad eggs' smell which mysteriously pervaded the chemistry lab whatever experiment had been undertaken could still be detected alongside the plaque - encapsulated for posterity! Perhaps our chemistry teacher 'Boggy Marsh' really did keep chickens in his store cupboard after all - it would certainly account for an awful lot!

By the time I had left school and had been training as an architect for two years the unthinkable happened in the historic heart of the city centre - wholesale clearance of much loved and well known landmarks and in fact whole streets making the city look more like a bomb site - something Hitler had not even managed to do! At the lower end of the city towards the river once stood the majestic Saracens Head - a cross between an hotel and a pub and proudly surmounted at eaves level by a fine bust of a middle eastern prince decked around with a crimson turban. Immediately opposite was one of the finest bakeries and it's obligatory restaurant all housed in a superb historic building; it recalled the days when Peterborough was a bustling market town with throngs of country folk enjoying themselves after selling their wares at the nearby markets. Next door was a solid yet utilitarian building which was home to the most amazing ironmongers - Petts. It was more akin to an aladdins cave and it would be safe to say it sold everything from a pin to a steamroller! Like the Swan public house that sported a fine shell porch and is now supplanted by a sports store in the Hereward Centre all were lost to the developers desire for new, bigger and supposedly better. Across from the Swan once stood the Waterloo Arcade built almost entirely of glass with cast iron columns, far in advance of it's day and from which was sold finest porcelain and china. Next door the sole remaining saddlers - it's home, a humble vernacular structure almost seemed out of place then, some 40 years ago! The loss of Campkins camera shop, a medieval timber framed building and now under the Long Causeway entrance to Queensgate shopping centre, was just as hard to accept. The Old Deaconian's Association annual dinners were often held in the Angel Hotel opposite the Town Hall where I remember the hostelry's wonderful interior - almost of a bygone era the opulent grand staircase rose gracefully to the Fitzwilliam Rooms. I already had a link with the Angel. As a teenager I would load up fruit and vegetables from the old stables at the rear into an old battered truck at some godforsaken time every Saturday morning in readiness for selling at the General Market. Both hotel and stables alongside Priestgate were swept away and replaced by a hideous brick and concrete edifice now occupied by W H Smith.

Towards the North Station the devastation was even more horrendous. The George Hotel, a distinctive 19th. Century building lying opposite the station and the scene of my 21st.birthday celebrations was flattened and even the Parish Burial Ground in existence since 1805 was lost under acres of concrete and tarmac to form a 'much needed' traffic interchange. Miraculously above all this carnage one little building, located in a street once renowned to be the Common Muckhill, remained isolated for many a month long after all it's neighbours had disappeared. The forlorn structure, a little garage complete with it's ancient pumps and nostalgic motor signs, defied all comers and continued to trade. Then one day it was no more - it had gone to the great big scrap heap in the sky! Close by but seemingly at a safer distance from the ever advancing machinery stood a terrace of unassuming, grim, dirty workers cottages no doubt first erected around 1850 at the time of the great railway development in the city. Their name, Sweet Briar Walk, has always stayed with me, although remembering their conditions and limited size living in them must have been anything but sweet! The garden was no more than a yard with a 10 foot high brick wall as a boundary to the nearby Wagon Works and sidings. Leaning up against the high wall each cottage had a wooden wash - house with a galvanised bathtub hanging from a rusty old nail on the flimsy door. Perhaps it was for the best that such conditions were not given a chance to remain.

In the years of destruction and upheaval I made a conscious effort to take a final lingering look at a fast disappearing part of what had once been a sleepy cathedral town with a fascinating historic centre. It was all captured on film and now resides in the City Museum as a record of what used to be.

When I felt saddened and confused at the mayhem I was witnessing there was only one place I headed for - through the Becket Chapel gateway into the precincts with the ancient cathedral as a backdrop. This still offers a tranquil haven of peace for all who seek to escape from the tumult of modern living. At the West end under the portrait of Robert Scarlett, a grave digger who buried two queens and the townsfolk twice over in his 98 years, the cool peace and impressive grandeur of the vast Norman cathedral is enhanced by the echoing tones of the organist practising for the forthcoming Easter services.

All is calm and the world seems at peace with itself. At least I can be certain that this will not be a memory of something lost forever.

Footnote: The Farrows factory site has now been totally cleared and yet more housing is rising out of the ground.

THINGS THAT GO BUMP IN THE NIGHT

Railway stations and those hissing monsters of steam, now sadly a fading memory, held a great fascination for me from a very early age. I'm sure I was no different to any other young boy bewitched by the magic of the 'iron road' but I was certainly more fortunate than many.

Across the road from our primary school and only a short walk from our house through overgrown allotments was the East Coast mainline awash with an amazing assortment of trains every few minutes. From main line expresses and stopping trains to fast fish trains, clanking old freights and pottering pick up goods - I could see them all! Who could wish for more? Truthfully I was spoilt for choice but I was far too young to appreciate that - I lived within 15 minutes walk of the crossroads of railway lines bringing trains from London, York, Doncaster, Edinburgh, Leeds, Crewe, Birmingham, Norwich, Lincoln and far beyond. At the centre of this 'spaghetti junction' lay two very busy stations, three large engine depots and a vast sprawling area of marshalling yards and sidings over which hung a blanket of haze and coal smoke that left in it's wake a layer of grime on all fixed and moveable objects. At night the lights of the yards and stations lit up the sky as if the whole city were ablaze and formed an eerie backdrop to the mighty Norman cathedral.

In primary school days I was restricted to watching trains from the comparative safety of the old allotment field, recording their numbers in my much prized spotters book. Was it a 'Streak','Jinty','Jubilee'.or Black 5? It was hardly surprising that intense competition developed between the spotters with notes being exchanged excitedly about the latest sighting and the securing of a long sought after engine number. On reaching Grammar School I found I could extend my range of operations and regular as clockwork met friends every Saturday morning at the old Fair Meadow, conveniently located between the intersection of all the lines entering the city. Nothing escaped us!

In my schoolboy days the railways were an everyday part of life whether you used them to reach school, college, work or the coast for a holiday. The network employed many thousands from the large city stations and termini through minor rural halts to engine depots, wagon works and marshalling yards. Wherever you went in town or country you bumped into railways. Some 30 years earlier in my father's schooldays the railways ruled supreme as the internal combustion engine had not yet taken an iron grip on the nation. School outings, most frequently to the seaside at Hunstanton or Skegness, provided all the pupils with a day out circumnavigating the hitherto little seen rural backwaters of British Railways whilst only allowing them limited time with buckets and spades on the beach - but of course the train ride was all part of the adventure! My father often recalled these 'red letter' days for the village children and vividly remembered the 'leader', a Sunday School teacher, imparting words of wisdom and warning in hushed tones to the assembled crowd as to the dangers that might befall a youngster on the journey. Imprinted on the minds of the pupils, almost as if it were a matter of life or death, was the time of departure from the seaside. The 'leader' ensured that no pupil was in doubt as to the consequences if they went missing at the crucial time! It is certain as night follows day that some boy would strike fear and panic into the 'leader' and cause the train and the whole party to be held up. As often as not the offender was most usually found on the station footbridge gazing with grubby, smutted face at the very train that was waiting for him! Whisked away unceremoniously he would be placed firmly in his carriage seat along with his bucket containing a very angry crab! Lost in clouds of steam the train nonchalantly and lazily chugged out of the station to wend it's way homeward with it's cargo of happy but worn out children. The 'leader' contented herself by dutifully reminding her charges that they should be counting the 'Nestles milk cows' in the fields - Friesians to us country folk! Oh for the innocence of childhood days.

By the end of my Grammar School days the steam railways were already in decline and the new fangled diesels were invading every part of the network even down to the smallest unmanned halt deep in the countryside. But to my friends and I the railways never lost their fascination. I had a long felt desire to know exactly what lay beyond the massive grime laden wall that ringed the huge main line engine depot in the city. All a small boy could see was a haze of smoke, the rooftops of the depot and a towering coaling plant with wagons ominously balanced as if in mid air halfway up it's sides. Playing football on Saturdays and Sundays in the New England area of the city offered me a more distant view of the smoke laden complex but of course I was concentrating on the game and running down that wing! Hitching a ride on the footplate of the Peterborough East Station pilot tank engine on it's seemingly endless journeys back and forth under the unusual 'high level' signal box from the carriage sidings was another 'must' in every railway mad schoolboys dreams.

I attained my 'goals' with some surprising ease and was able to boast my achievements to schoolmates whilst dreaming of yet more adventures to come.

Late one evening however there came an almighty bang and the sound of tearing metal from the direction of the main line. It was not until the following morning that the full consequences of the 'bump in the night' became apparent. Piled high in a tangled mess of wagon sides, wheels, rails and masses of ballast lay the remnants of an unfitted freight train complete with it's untouched engine from the local depot simmering impatiently at the front. Chaos reigned for some days whilst the carnage was removed and the track reinstated. The engine made it's way back almost forlornly to the yards to select some 'sensible' and 'friendly' wagons that wouldn't play tricks and was seen a few days later quite happily working it's way up the freight lines towards London again. Reflecting on the incident it could quite easily have been Henry or

Gordon, the friends of Thomas the Tank Engine! Normal service was resumed.

Such excitement can't last forever but you can still dream despite looming 'A' level exams, the inexorable wait for the results and the euphoria of beckoning University life or shattering disappointment at a return to that dreaded exam room. Maybe failure in the 'A' levels would mean a return to my beloved railways and more opportunities to watch my favourite local football team, the Posh, in action.

On a bitterly cold winters night I would often stay awake peering through my 'frosted' bedroom window to the clear moonlit sky and listening to the friendly bump and clank of wagons being shunted in the yards under glistening crystal lights. While attempting to work out some form or pattern to the frost on my window I would await the expected 'toot' from the shunting engine as it reported it's intentions and movements to the men with shunting poles walking between the rakes of wagons. By morning, with alarm clock ringing in my ears calling me to breakfast and the sun not yet risen from it's own slumbers, the bumps of the night had stopped and some 50 or more freight trains had left for every corner of the country. The night's unseen work had been done.

There are no longer any bumps in the night - they are but just memories of a bygone era.

ADESTE FIDELES

The week before Christmas was the most hectic yet enjoyable in our grammar school calendar.

As choristers for the school at St. John's Parish Church in the heart of the ancient city we were expected to give up our time to practice until perfect for the Festival of Nine Lessons and Carols to be held in the candlelit church on the final day of term. Many of our school friends thought it must be a chore but they didn't know what they were missing! My first day of the last week of term started just as the remaining four were to be - peddle furiously through the city to school for assembly, spend a couple of hours in my form doing nothing in particular only to be released by the master, in front of envious classmates, for school choir duty. How we used to love watching their long faces as we loaded up our satchels onto the crossbars of our bikes and headed off the to the Parish Church. Once in the 6th.form and a prefect we had the privilege of going direct to the church for 1 o'clock practice and did not even attend school - we felt highly honoured.

Practices in the church under the watchful eye of Mr Warner, the Music Master, were strict yet good humoured and we were always made to feel that little bit more important than those languishing at school - normally we were rewarded with finishing just before light fall at about 4 o'clock. I shall always remember leaving my bike propped up against the South Aisle wall, opening the massive oak door to the West tower and entering the softly lit church whilst the organist practised gentle and echoing Christmas music; the lofty Christmas tree by the north door glistened and sparkled with it's many lights. With the heavy door closed behind me shutting out the bitter cold air of the gathering winter afternoon I was enveloped in the warmth and glow of the ancient church. As always the church gave up a 'spirit of place' - it was a good feeling - warm and welcoming. We always enjoyed our practices in this wonderful building perhaps because our music master felt relaxed within these ancient but most friendly of walls - there was certainly a great sense of 'belonging' and it must have made all the difference to us. The only other time I can recall experiencing anything at all like this was on the several occasions I was called on to play the organ at our local Methodist Chapel for midnight service on Christmas Eve. Truthfully it never attained the elevated heights of our practices and Festival of Carols at St. Johns.

The highlight even of the practices was my form friend 'Bloggs' Richardson's rendition of the first verse of Once in Royal David's City. His treble voice was near nigh perfect and could match any of the choristers at Kings College, Cambridge. His solo in the Festival on the last day of term was truly angelic and was complimented so wonderfully by the choristers turned out in red and white cassocks and surplices and carrying flickering candles. It was certainly some spectacle for parents and friends 'packed to the rafters' in the church.

Sadly, but inevitably, Bloggs suddenly discovered one day during choir practice in the Music Room that he could no longer reach the 'idyllic heights' - he had overnight, like me, been converted to an alto and later baritone and bass! Bloggs' reign as soloist was over and he joined me on the second row of the choir stalls, elevated to a far more important role - singing bass or baritone and trying to keep the 1st and 2nd form choristers in order! The deep hidden recesses of the choir stalls were a golden invitation to any young boy to carry out pranks - avoiding the gaze of Mr Warner furiously waving his baton while the organ scholar plied his trade on the ivories was not easy but certainly a challenge! Paper pellets formed out of surplus choir sheets were flicked across the chancel at opposing choristers and even paper aeroplanes found themselves gliding gracefully across the church that is, until the music master turned to find a projectile flying directly at him! Choristers, always so easy to adapt, promptly turned to seeing how far they could pass sticky sweets down the stalls until they became 'impassable'. Unfortunately on one occasion a young 'unhardened' 2nd former forgot who was seated next to him and handed the by now extremely sticky sweet to the Science Master who was, at the very moment, concentrating hard on a difficult bass part. The consequences were highly embarrassing for the master but sent the boys into hilarious fits of laughter promptly bringing the practice to a sudden end! Fortunately for the 2nd former he had deposited the sweet on the master's seat where a sheet of music lay; picking the sheet up and placing it below others in his hand for later use the master suddenly became aware he could not separate any of his sheets. Confusion reigned and the bass input immediately dried up much to the mystification of the music master! Somehow the science master bumbled his way through the remainder of the carol and sat down red faced and confused! Nothing was ever discovered or said!

Handing in our Carol Sheets and picking up our satchels we left the warmth and glow of the old church by the tower doorway to find ourselves in the narrow passage next to the Corn Exchange. Sadly, as many of my age will know, this rather fine edifice succumbed like many of the older buildings in the city to be replaced by a monolithic concrete and glass office block that is a scar on the townscape and St. Johns Parish Church. As so often after choir practice we walked into a crisp, frosty early winter evening with rime covered streets and roofs and a stupendous blood orange sunset. Alongside the church the stark skeletal remnants of street traders stalls were silhouetted against the clear evening sky as fishmongers and butcher's assistants attempted to wash down the street and pavement before it froze like a sheet of ice. I would walk my bike past the shops in Church Street and Market Square, now glowing with warm light in the fast ebbing daylight, and pause in the centre of the cobbled market place to gaze upon the Gates Memorial - a High Gothic monument erected to Henry Pearson Gates, the Dean and Chapter's High Bailiff and first Mayor of the Borough. Today, the cobbled market place has been swept away along with the general market and the Gates Memorial - the general market now boasts a modern building at the north end of the city close to the old Embassy Theatre whilst the Memorial has long since been removed stone by stone to the Bishops Gardens, amidst a sea of flowers, on the southern edge of the Cathedral precincts. Curiously the Market Place or Market Hill was renamed Cathedral Square by the City Council presumably because they had removed the market and all it's bustle and activity - the square no longer has the character and presence despite the stunning backdrop of the 17th.century Butter Cross and the ancient Becket Gateway to the Cathedral.

Picking my way around fruiterers and florist's boxes scattered at the base of the Gates Memorial I would turn eastwards towards the Becket Gateway. A few people, huddled in heavy coats, hats and scarves against the biting cold, hurried through the gateway about their business - their hunched bodies silhouetted against the eerie glow of a single lantern set just inside the archway. They vanished as fast as they had appeared into the gathering gloom of the precincts as if they had never been. The city was closing down for the day. Above the gateway the ghostly image of the great West front began to emerge lit only by the fast setting sun and the glow of the meagre precinct lights - the cathedral almost looked as though it was on fire! An awesome sight!

I would mount my bike and steer a course down the now brightly lit main thoroughfare, Bridge Street, past the elegant Town Hall and the many shopkeepers closing up having decided there was little trade left to bother about. Past the old Custom House and the river bridge I finally reached the highest point of my journey on the very top of the East Station Bridge just as a train left in a cloud of steam for Northampton, Rugby or Leicester. Once the steam had cleared ahead I could see the football stadium and it's floodlight pylons and beyond in the southern suburb of Peterborough, the haze and glow of the many brickworks chimneys, still spewing their 'filth' into the oncoming night sky. My friends headed home to the northern outskirts of the city whilst I peddled furiously towards Fletton. A hard frost was on the cards.

What of the Festival of Nine Lessons and Carols? As always it was a great success and a wonderful celebration of the Feast of Christmas to come. We reverently sang many of our carols in Latin although I'm sure few of us fully understood the true meaning. My old headmaster attempted to teach me the rudiments of the language but with little end result judging by the 0 out of 20 for my class tests!

'Zeroid boy!' was his shout as my homework book came flying across the classroom!

It was good fun.

Adeste fideles laeti triumphantes.

WHERE'S YOUR GLASSES?

One warm May evening the family found itself alongside a hundred or so committed souls supporting and cheering on the local football team in their endeavours against the 'steelmen' of Ebbw Vale. It was a far cry even from the 2nd and 3rd divisions of the Football League and even more so from the exalted heights of the Arsenal at the mighty Highbury Stadium.

A member of the family stood out for reasons of his apparel - our youngest son, David, was kitted out in black and white striped shirt ready to do battle in an under 9's representative match during half time. Some may scoff at the attempts of these youngsters but it must be said they are totally committed to the game for the duration and they don't get paid! They just play for the love of the game which is more than can be said for many of the professionals who, it must be admitted, may only have a limited time 'at the top'.

Once young David had completed his match I went 'backstage' to help with his kit and was amazed at the conditions that met my eye in the changing rooms. They were not far off the privation suffered by many a small village club similar to the team for which my father and his brother played in the 30's. To gain entry you had to circumnavigate the rusting hulk of the remnants of a bicycle parked unceremoniously in the passage. It looked as if the 'machine' had not moved in years. What was its purpose and what had happened to it's no doubt illustrious rider? I never found out. The general tenure of the place was down at heel, dingy and certainly not the place in which to 'lift the spirits' of those that needed lifting be they the home or visiting sides. As with the vast majority of small clubs 'spare' money is at a premium and teams and their managers would be the first to admit they rely heavily on the goodwill and support of a few hardy, willing helpers and supporters and - bless them - the tea ladies. Village and small town football would not be the same without them - if the truth were to be told they have 'hearts of gold' supplying the heavenly nectar whatever the weather.

The village team my father and his brother played for, Warboys Town, were not endowed with vast financial resources and were a true community effort in ever respect, home or away. I am told some of the players met in one of the many village pubs, the Rose and Crown in the High Street, where they changed in the pub rooms before venturing out onto the pitch often meeting the remainder of the team already kitted out, who had cycled long distances to play. No lack of commitment in this team! The proximity of pub to pitch was no accident either although players couldn't go far wrong wherever they played their matches in the village - there were so many pubs! Spectators were charged the princely sum of 3d for entry, tendering their hard earned money to a club official who sat in a ramshackle one seater wooden hut. So tight was the fit it can only be assumed the official had but little choice to walk to the pub for his beverage in his 'mobile house' and be assisted out by willing helpers. There was certainly little chance of an armed raid in the circumstances! The highlight of the football calendar in the village was as always the local 'derby' matches with Somersham and Ramsey when caution was thrown to the wind to secure a much coveted win and, of course, the visit by one of the up and coming clubs in the preliminary round of the F.A Amateur Cup. Only too often the village team, having held the opposition in front of their own highly partisan crowd, were then flattened and swept out of sight in the replay when the 'giants' triumphed over the 'minnows'. Like the village feast the cup match was seen as a high day and holiday not to be missed for all the carrots and sugar beet in the fens. My father quite readily recalled as a youngster being walked some 3 miles from the fens into the village by a carrot digger and her husband to see the 'match of the year'. Having consumed a hearty meal of sausage and mash they then returned the 3 miles at the dead of night to arrive home at 1 in the morning. My father and his brother thought this a wonderful treat!

Some 30 years or more later in the early 60's I experienced as a young lad the same highs and lows when I was regularly taken by my father to see our 'new' local heroes do battle on a Saturday afternoon. The 'Posh', as they were known, had been 'demolishing' all - comers in the Midland League for more years than their supporters could recall and had been knocking loud and clear on the door of the Football League seeking acknowledgement for their heroic deeds. I, like the rest of the supporters, felt totally let down when the team could only manage 6 goals with no reply against teams with fascinating names such as Blyth Spartans, Frickley Athletic and Spennymoor United. We thought the world of our team - Derek Dougan, Terry Bly, Peter

MacNamee and Norman Rigby just to name a few - and their daring F A Cup giant killing exploits. Many a time famous clubs such as Arsenal, Crystal Palace and Aston Villa must have quaked in their shoes on receiving 'the call' to London Road to meet the 'Posh'. They must have feared for their very beings at the thought of a fired up partisan crowd and team with nothing to lose but with a sole purpose in life - to humiliate them and put them out of the cup!

The match against the mighty Arsenal at London Road in front of a seething crowd of 27000 must rank as the player's 'finest hour and a half'. Despite the whole of the Arsenal team, apart from their goalkeeper being encamped in the Posh goalmouth for the last quarter of an hour our team came through 2-1 winners. So packed was the ground that my father was unable to take his hands out of his pockets due to the pressure of people on every side! This victory must even outshine the teams valiant 1-1 draw with Aston Villa in the London Road 'mudbath' - it was almost impossible to pick out who was playing for whom in the torrential rain and liquid mud although our Jim Rayner, just discernable in his blue and white, played his heart out defying anything the Villa could throw at him. Sadly these days can never be repeated - but quite rightly as far as safety is concerned. Since the Hillsborough disaster safety has become paramount and ground capacities have dropped in the wake of developing all seater stadium with a greater emphasis on accommodating families and providing facilities for a day out at the 'big match'. However nothing can take away the memory of that unique thrill and experience of being part of such a vast heaving mass of humanity urging their team on to greater glory. The little brown painted stool that went with me to every match was placed, almost ceremoniously, behind the boundary wall of the Glebe Road terraces could tell a tale or two if it were still around! How could I forget the players in their famous blue and white strip running onto the pitch supported by 'Mr Posh' dressed in top hat and tails, ringing a bell and carrying a walking cane. The whole ensemble was accompanied by a rendition of the Post Horn Gallop blaring forth from the loudspeaker system; it was a sight that lifted the spirit of the fans and spurred the players to even greater heights. The noise that emanated from the ground on match days was deafening and even though we lived a mile from the ground we were left in no doubt when the Posh had scored. A copy of the Pink 'Un paper that evening confirmed another success!

My youngest son now reminds me that we support the Arsenal as well as the Posh, just as his Grandad did, and he dreams of meeting his heroes at London Road and Highbury in the near future. Like all football mad boys he now sports replica Arsenal and Posh shirts and idolises his favourite players - the Arsenal and England goalkeeper David Seaman, who, I am constantly reminded began his career with the Posh and his opposite number at Posh the fabulous Mark Tyler. Of course I must not forget our local team, Carmarthen Town, valiantly flying the flag in the League of Wales along with their junior sides being groomed for bigger and better dreams - possibly at the famous Old Trafford? They can but dream.

How did our youngest son fare in his match and few minutes of glory in front of a hundred or so partisan and no doubt knowledgeable fans? It was a goal less draw but not surprisingly without incident as both teams strived to break a nail biting deadlock. A near miss by David's forward colleagues on the opponents' goal had been marred by an untidy and clumsy tackle on the edge of the penalty area. It left a youngster flattened on the pitch well after the melee of players, which seemed to be the aggregate of both teams, had moved on like a mass of swarming bees down the pitch to confront David, a sole defender, and his diminutive keeper. As if on recall of the penalty area incident an older spectator close by suddenly jumped up, as the stadium fell silent for a crucial free kick, and exclaimed in a broad Welsh accent 'Where's your glasses ref?'

The player miscued his free kick to the great delight of David and his team and the match was finished to shouts of appreciation. Perhaps justice was done. Well done lads - you did us proud.

Convenient the referee couldn't see!

The "Four Gentlemen" at the Triangular Bridge, Crowland

The Weir,
Warboys

Site of North Station, Ramsey

*Old River Nene
at Ugg Mere, Ramsey,
St. Mary's*

The Methodist Chapel and White Hart, Warboys

Whittlesey Mere, Holme Fen Nature Reserve

The Fen Posts, Holme Fen Nature Reserve

*Holme Lode near Tower Farm,
Holme Fen Nature Reserve*

Meeting of Old Nene and Whittlesey Dike, Flood's Ferry

Waterloo Arcade, Peterborough

Sweet Briar Walk, Peterborough

*Old Deacon's School
and Perkins Factory,
Deacon Street, Peterborough*

*St. John's Church
and White Horse,
Peterborough*

The Apple Harvest

Peterborough. Market Place.

933

St. John's Church, Guildhall and Gates Memorial in the Market Place, c. 1906, Peterborough

A class V2 heads for King's Cross above the Fair Meadow, Peterborough

PETERBOROUGH UNITED F.C,
FOURTH DIVISION CHAMPIONS 1960-1961
BACK WHITTAKER RIPLEY WALLS WALKER BLY RAYNER
FRONT HAILS EMERY RIGBY SMITH McNAMEE

Peterborough Utd. F.C. 1960-61 Squad, Champions of Football League Division 4

Peterborough Cathedral

III

FENLAND
ADVENTURE

BRIGHT AND CRISP AND UNEVEN

Silhouetted against a bright crisp winter afternoon sky a solitary figure went about his labours in a vast unending field of sugar beet with no trees, hedge or building in sight. His rusty old bike lay against the fast decaying remnants of a five - barred gate which strangely had no fencing to accompany it and stood isolated by the side of the muddy fen track as if left as a reminder of what used to be. Talk to any old fen farmhand and he would see nothing out of the ordinary with this gate nor with the wild flat inhospitable landscape - it's always been like this since time began so why try to change it?

As I was about to move on in an attempt to defrost my body my eye was diverted back to the labourer, dressed in grubby overcoat tied together with twine, and now struggling across the field in the teeth of a bitterly cold wind. His approach was painfully slow but the first words he uttered in a broad fen accent as he walked by me, as if I didn't exist, were not unexpected.

'W'ere d'yew come from?'

Conversation with fen folk is nothing if not blunt, short and to the point. Once satisfied I was from the same town he stared into the distance away across the field in which he had been working all day and considered his position with some deliberation. The next question was just as blunt and obvious.

'Then whot yew doin' 'ere?'

The straightness of his question took me aback although I had no excuse considering my frequent encounters with the old gentlemen that spent most of their day chewing the cud under the butter cross in the town. It was a valid enquiry but still very difficult to answer adequately to these wily and stubborn old fenman. Having spun him a plausible yarn about my deep interest in sugar beet and it's tending before the fast approaching harvest he seemed reasonably satisfied and at ease and shuffled across to his old bike. Lifting a massive army greatcoat from the intrepid machine he produced a greaseproof wrapped packet tied awkwardly together with fraying string and promptly lowered himself to the ground to consume his 'docky' under the shelter of the coat.

I watched, dumbstruck, in complete silence. Nothing was said and nothing happened except for the occasional moan of the wind and the rustling of the reeds in the dyke by the gate. 'Docky' finished he raised himself, placing the crumpled greaseproof paper wrapping and string into a cavernous pocket, picked up his well used wooden handled hoe, mounted the rusting steed and squeaked off down the track. Not a word was uttered. I pinched myself out of the trance that had fallen over me and gazed back towards the town and the direction in which the old farmhand had travelled. He was but a black speck on the horizon heading for home and a welcoming fire into which he would most likely stare long and silently - his routine had come with long practice ever since he had automatically become a labourer on the local farm since leaving school as a teenager.

Venturing back to the town, still rapped deep in thought, I headed for the market square and the old butter cross. The sun by now was falling rapidly in the west and although the fens have no hills to obliterate it's warmth and welcoming presence St. Mary's Church, the fine Georgian building housing the Post Office and the George Pubic House bordering the Market Place cast deep shadows across the square causing a deep chill to descend. The market traders although well protected from the insidious cold by layers of clothing and the ubiquitous fingerless gloves began to seriously consider calling it a day. Under the fine pyramidal roof of the butter cross sat a group of hardy old timers drawing on their weather beaten pipes and exchanging stories of days gone by - and no doubt today's problems. Some of them I'm sure remembered as children the infamous Pentecostal preacher who spat fire and brimstone at bemused fen workers from a farm cart purloined for the purpose from the backyard of a pub fringing the market place. Protected by thick woolly scarves and gloves the old men recalled past days of working the land in unbelievably bitter winters when the Whittlesey Washes of the Nene set as hard as iron as the harsh weather continued for week after week. One old gentleman, propping his arched body on a rustic wooden stick joked and reminisced of the almost festive skating competitions held on the deep frozen waters. As snow settled on the fields and severe frosts set in thousands of land workers out of work on account of the arctic conditions took to the ice along with strange Heath - Robinsonish contraptions which spewed and belched great black clouds of smoke through a tall stove pipe like chimney and yet produced, we are told, the finest fish and chips in the land! How these cauldrons of heat and steam managed not to sink through the ice is still a mystery; presumably their intrepid owners had some intimate knowledge as to when they had to make their escape to terra firma. For many years at the turn of the 20th.century competitive speed skating in the Fens, where many a reputation was won and lost, was the highlight of the year. Memories obviously still lingered on in the old gentlemen - names such as Turkey Smart and Charlie Tebbutt could be heard in their conversation.

Talking is thirsty work and as if on the click of a switch they all raised their weary bodies and headed on automatic pilot straight for one of the pubs. As drawn by a magnet I followed ever more eager to hear of past brave deeds by their colleagues some of whom no doubt had already been called to a 'better life' above. With beer in their bellies they began to argue over the awesome reputation held by the town.

'Without a word of a lie' one said 'there was a day when there was a different pub for each week and that's as true as I stand here'.

His friends did not seem at all surprised at his forceful and apparently accurate statement and in fact continued in the same vein eulogising on how you could stay in the bar of a pub for a whole week to have a 'good drink' and of the time when pubs began to be named after the letters of the alphabet since they were so short of names! Plied with copious amounts of alcohol they then began to recall times when they or a friend attempted to overcome notorious '18 pint a night characters' who frequently finished up returning home in a 'borrowed' wheelbarrow! Almost unbelievable stories of men who, having consumed as much as 2 gallons of beer, were still able to hit the bullseye of the dartboard time after time, began permeating the jovial discourse. Some digressed onto stories of ghosts and apparitions seen wandering the fen village streets late at night. One haunting in particular seemed to attract a great deal of attention from all closely gathered around the bar. It seemed that a white hooded figure had been observed leading a ghostly grey horse and cart festooned with flickering lights - most likely the night soil cart!

'I was frit'r death' exclaimed the narrator visibly shaking - he had obviously been deeply moved!

'Nothing more thun that 'ol ruffian Tommy Onyett in a white sheet' retorted a younger man.

At this the group erupted into raucous laughter and the glasses clanked and jangled on the bar at the noise. At this juncture as the laughter reached a crescendo and several of my 'friends' appeared decidedly unsteady I discreetly stepped out of the pub into what was now a bright and crisp winter evening. Lights were already on in the street and nearby shops and looking upwards at the ancient hostelry I cast my eyes on the pub sign - I had been drinking at the Letter B! Suddenly the tales of those old fenmen did not seem so far fetched and incredulous.

Feeling decidedly unsteady - or was the footpath that uneven as it appeared to be rising up to meet me - I cautiously headed home a wiser man.

IS THERE A FIREMAN ANYWHERE?

A blood red sun was setting gently in the west over Clare Country – the low heaths and woodland around Ufford, Helpston and Southey and Lady Woods – on a pleasantly warm and peaceful late summer evening.

The final stretch of my walk would bring me from the delightful village of Etton, with it's glorious medieval church opposite the Elizabethan Manor House and it's 'his and hers' privy, across the old fashioned railway crossing near Woodcroft Castle and towards my 'goal' – the Green Man pub at Marholm. I allowed my thoughts to wander in the pleasing warmth as the village and pub came into view across the now golden coloured fields as the sun prepared to 'tuck itself up in bed'. But surely that was not a tree in the nearby field? Suddenly I was awoken from my dreamy thoughts; I swiftly stepped into the middle of the lane and concentrated my view across a field that had recently been stripped of its crop of wheat. An isolated, silhouetted figure was marching across the field swinging something akin to a long pole in front of him. Occasionally he would stop, bend down, pluck what appeared to be a long handled trowel from his side and dig feverishly – then he would resume marching across the field having placed something in a shoulder bag. I stood transfixed for what seemed a lifetime until my mind kicked into gear! It was an infidel – a metal detector!

In the 1960's and 70's when the city of Peterborough had been designated a New Town, a professional archaeology unit, Nene Valley Archaeology, was set up to investigate potentially important sites that might succumb to development. Individuals and groups of metal detectors were then regarded as a major threat since they removed 'items' completely out of context and with no relationship to archaeological layers and historical occupation. Many of the 'items' never even saw the light of day and some perpetrators even forgot where they had dug up a fine Bronze Age Axe!

Many people had a great desire to be directly involved in discovering and uncovering the past and longed to have a 'hands on' approach; sadly they were unable to join professional units. Around 1980, having been directly involved in major archaeological work in Norfolk, I decided something had to be done and North Cambs. Archaeological Unit was born!

As well as enabling enthusiasts to undertake minor site excavations 'in context' it also added considerably to local knowledge, offered 'education' to the general public and was an excellent social meeting point. Over 10 years or so the Unit, supported by a hard core of workers who braved every conceivable condition, worked on many Medieval and Roman sites in the Peterborough area. The Unit even created a 'live' excavation at the East of England Show for many years and were honoured to have Princess Anne {now the Princess Royal} and the Duke of Gloucester visit 'the site' – we almost persuaded the Duke to be both Patron and a worker!

The final triumph came in 1987 when the unit were asked to help excavate a site near the city centre which was to be subjected to housing development. The professional body, Nene Valley Archaeology, chose the higher ground around what was known to be the site of the church as they considered this would proffer the best results. Our little unit were allocated the lower and supposedly less interesting 'domestic' site. Oh how the professionals were disappointed – they uncovered little of any note! What a set of results for the amateur team – footprints of Saxon timber framed dwellings complete with their hearths and rubbish pits and amazingly Prehistoric round huts! Once the importance of our finds had been established we had to become 'infidels' – we used metal detectors at the close of each working day to ensure that any true 'infidel' would not wreak havoc by leaving the site looking as though moles had been searching for a mate!! Such was the enthusiasm within the unit that one of the team, Ron, a fireman, persuaded his bosses to allow him to bring their Simon Snorkel onto site – on 'test'! The view for the team from 100 feet in the air was amazing – it put the icing on the cake!

Celebrations in the form of a barbeque took place on the site and Ron volunteered to set up the grill and charcoal on the extremity of the excavations and ensure it was well alight for cooking the 'goodies' Ron then took off across the site to talk to some of the visitors.

Calm overtook the site as workers and visitors consumed food and drink until suddenly a cry went up – someone had noticed that the hawthorn hedge next to the barbeque was well alight with flames leaping skywards!

The call went up –

'Is there a fireman anywhere?'

SOMETHING NASTY IN THE WOODSHED

Having visited, inspected and minutely investigated many ancient houses across the country in the course of my work I feel I can safely say that I have an empathy for the atmosphere and presence of these 'living' structures. The old saying 'If only these walls could talk' is far nearer the truth than many realise or would care to accept. It is a commonly held belief supported by many of the professionals in the field that the presence of a 'being' can be retained in footwear and footwear alone - hence the strong superstitious rights attached to the shoe in all parts of the kingdom. Strangely it is far more difficult for people to accept and recognise that buildings can retain the presence of good or evil doings just as many have scoffed at my ability, given by whom I'm not sure, to divine for water with stainless steel rods or hazel twigs. Whether we like it or not buildings and even land can possess a spirit of people and events long since forgotten or lost in history and we ignore it at our peril! Not everyone who has experienced a 'presence' or observed a 'being' could be classified as either disturbed or deliberately distorting the truth in order to gain publicity or notoriety. Below the streets of London in the underground, on the field which saw the Battle of Naseby or in some country manor house or humble farm building there are secret tales to tell and hints of strange happenings, most of which can quite often be rationally explained.

Some years ago I directed a small group of amateur enthusiasts as an archaeology unit, the North Cambridgeshire Archaeology Group, investigating minor sites on the very edge of the Fens - a land steeped in mystery, superstition and much untold fascinating history. The unit had a particular interest in what could be classified as a minor Roman Road, the Fen Causeway, although reflecting upon it now it's importance and relevance to the region's development all those years ago must have been far greater than we could ever appreciate. Sadly the route of the old road had been neglected by the professional archaeologists in favour of juicier pickings since it's physical presence remained very low key. Quite often only located by a faint crop mark the road 'marched' across hostile terrain hopping from island to island leaving evidence of settlements at the most sizeable safe passing places and giving access during the 'dry season' for the passage of a Roman legionary cohort from a station in the east to a Roman town in the uplands to the west. Many a disaster must have struck on this road even in the dry months despite the best precautions.

As always ancient and historic sites are often reused time and time again and one such was the centre of our study by the Unit even though the old farmhouse, close to Coates and the ancient watercourse Morton's Leam, was found to be no more than 275 years old. Knowing the old buildings stood by the side of the route of the Roman Road, had been empty for some 30 odd years and now saw service as a farm store, did not raise any suspicions. Entry told my companion's dog and me that this was not a happy place but for whatever reason it remained a mystery for some time. With the dog howling and refusing to enter one of the bedrooms at the head of the main staircase and avoiding one of the dilapidated outbuildings across the overgrown yard my feelings were confirmed - there was certainly a 'cold and unwelcoming' if not downright evil atmosphere which left me totally uneasy. It was only later when one of the team happened to talk to the farm owner and mention in passing the strange events that had taken place when we had entered the building that everything became clear. In Edwardian times a daughter of the then farmer, a Mr Flint, had been promised in marriage to a local farmhand who, on being called up for service in the army, was lost, presumed dead. From hearing the news of her loss the daughter found she could not console herself and remained committed to her room - the very bedroom - until totally distraught, she took her own life. Some years later her father could no longer stand the strain and hung himself in the outbuilding.

'Not a happy building, eh?' said the farmer one day on calling to see us working.

'Sum 'ave ev'n seen the gal's ghost at the top o' them stairs - an' her pet dog as well. Mind you o'ive never been privy to it!'

Watching with great intensity one of our team carefully picking their way around a large shard of pottery he continued.

'My mother an' her gran'mother refused to live here. Who can blame 'em? You'm can see why the 'ol place has been empty ever since!'

Our team pondered his eloquent dialogue for some considerable time as he slowly wandered from the excavation performing his walk as slowly as possible as if to emphasise the gravity of what he had just said. Almost as he reached the privy at the end of the outbuilding range he stopped in his tracks as if he had been struck by a sudden thought or concern over what he had already told us. As if to emphasise the mystery of the place he slowly turned round, eyed us all as if we were about to unearth one of the victims, and lugubriously said

'Some even ses they'm seen one of them Roman soldiers or summat roide past this 'ol place on horseback - yeah, 'an with 'is shield and sword!'

It wasn't long after that the team decided to call it a day with the excavations at Flint Farm; few, including myself, were inclined to go through the experience witnessed once more. We might have bumped into that Roman soldier on horseback and he could well have been unfriendly!

What of the excavations on this ancient site? Very little and certainly no sign of foul deeds, that is, if you don't classify the skeleton of a wild boar as suspicious! As one of the older members of the team sagely pronounced 'It's best to let sleeping dogs lie'.

But be warned wherever you are - there could be something nasty in that thar' woodshed!

GOD'S IN HIS ELEMENT

There is little more daunting than the unending flatness of the Fens particularly when God has decided to wreak havoc with an unforgiving north easterly gale straight out of the North Sea. Even the hardiest of souls would find this phenomenon hard to bear rather believing vengeance was being extracted for some past misdemeanours. The very first day I had seen Tudor Farm in it's last vestiges of life I had already travelled across the Fen wastes in the teethe of such a gale and horizontal rain that hit the car as if it were loaded with nails. Could anything be worse or more disheartening?

The journey from March - dispiritingly grey under leaden skies and now bereft of its once heralded sprawling marshalling yards, recently replaced by an uninspiring 'state of the art' prison - across hostile and unforbidding fen to the quaint but sleepy village of Benwick was unnerving. That most of Benwick's houses tilt precariously into the unforgiving peat soils leaves you thinking that you had one too many beers for lunch! I strained to pick out useful roadside features amidst the swirling rain and mist that engulfed the car as I tentatively drove along narrow roads that skirted the murky steel grey waters of the Old River Nene. Not at Pillard's Corner, Botany Bay or Floods Ferry did I once rise more than a metre above sea level - and there was nothing between me and those icy cold waters! The consequences of making a mistake were just too awful to contemplate. How could anyone live in this environment without ending it all?

Heading south, thankfully away from the river, and feeling somewhat relieved, I travel out across Benwick Mere, Puddock Bridge, Tick and Turf Fens in the mistaken belief that the worst is over. A five mile stretch of unbroken flat and arrow straight road lies ahead as the rain once more lashes viciously against my vehicle. Just as a mirage in the desert, a ghost like, forlorn and wind lashed pub suddenly appears out of the gloom - there is no sign of life and I'm not at all surprised. According to my friend in the nearby village of Warboys the pub was once called the Five Chimneys but is now the White Swan. As I scan my road map I discover to my horror that I have dropped to sea level - I start to pray for some dry weather and even a lifebelt should the sea decide to appear! Relief I am certain must be close at hand a few miles distant once I can reach the next village sited on an eminence one can only describe as a 'mountain' amidst a vast sea of nothing. That it is my old home village of Warboys is security enough even in such foul weather. As the car struggles up the side of the 'mountain' into the Mill End of the village at the dizzy height of 25m I pass the site of the station and the old brickworks where the once common 'whites' were made alongside the orange clay land drains. Today we use plastic for land drains and the old skills practised at these works have long since been forgotten. Both station and brickworks, once so central to the village's life, have long since gone although the house where I lived for the first 5 years of my life still stands side by side with others of it's ilk overlooking the old carrot washery and the bleak fenland beyond.

Suddenly the appalling weather seems less important as I slowly drive down the High Street past village pond, ironmongers shop, the 'mightier than thou' red brick Baptist Chapel, the humble Methodist Chapel, the old village school and the house where my grandparents once lived. Little has changed since I spent just 1 year in the Primary School that has now been converted gracefully into the library. The old Lodge House is unrecognisable after it's murderous desecration in the 60's but the Methodist Chapel is steadfastly the same with it's well manicured display of red roses set within a circular gravel bed in front of it's apsed end. Is that notice board the very same one I remember as a child? The message ' God be with you' emblazoned to one side in large red letters seemed very familiar. I could have quite easily sped down the recently 'created' by -pass but somehow I couldn't be bothered preferring to soak myself in total and fulfilling nostalgia. Past the large blue doors that once marked the site of the village bus company, the fish and chip shop, the butchers and the post office where once the portly and jovial owner regularly stood watching the world go by. I glance at the incongruous Victorian Clock Tower and travel on down an almost imperceptible hill past the steeple of the parish church and the grand red brick rectory set aloof in it's impressive grounds and meander once more into the nothingness - not this time of the fens but the site of the 2nd. World War airfield that saw so much joy, fear and sadness some 60 years ago. The break from village to airfield is so instantaneous -

almost painful. Peace and unhurried harmony are replaced by jarring, lifeless nothingness totally unlike the bleakness of the fens. As a very young boy revisiting my early haunts I can readily remember the burnt out skeletal remains of a wartime plane left, like some hideous modern sculpture, part hidden under thickets of brambles, by the road opposite the lychgate to the cemetery. Was there some hidden meaning here or was this just pure coincidence? This barren landscape now littered with the remains of hangers and weed-strewn runways has no place for me.

I implore my old car to rid me of this sad place and seek out quieter more agreeable backwaters in my ultimate quest to see Tudor Farm. There seemed little chance in the weather conditions that I would pick out the tarpaulin covered wreck as I steadily dropped down towards the old town nestled on the banks of the languid River Ouse. But fortune often favours the brave - there for all to see was a bright blue tarpaulined building sitting amidst a mass of anonymous housing. It just had to be Tudor Farm! It is one thing to recognise the purpose of your visit from a distance but it is another in reaching your goal around seemingly endless one - way systems and bypasses. Many years ago, when bypasses and ring roads were in their infancy, I remember the effort I expounded in attempting to circumnavigate a certain town by the name of Banbury. To this day I am quite certain all road signs directed me to Brackley or Daventry with not even a hint of Chipping Norton - the very place I needed to reach! Little has changed and it was more by luck than judgement that I found the old farmhouse after a great deal of head scratching by the locals.

'You'm in the wrong place'.

'You've got me thar'.

'You'm cud' troi' down that thar' lane'.

'Yew sure you'm git the roit' town?'

'What you'm a looki' for such a place in this weather? I wouldn't stay round 'ere at noit'.

What confidence builders! I seem to discuss the merits of every known cure for all diseases that can afflict animals and humans, what fruits of the field and hedgerow make potent wine strong enough to blow your brains out, create scrumptious jam and, of course, cure your warts and arthritis but still fail to reach any conclusion as to the whereabouts of the old building. Salvation suddenly arrives in the unlikely form of an obviously frustrated mother attempting to lead a belligerent little boy home from school under the shelter of a tattered umbrella which appears to have suffered most severely at the hands of ' im up thar'. With water streaming down her face and off her shiny blue mac she pointed to the wreck of a building just 200 yards away!

I am stunned that it is not better known even if only for it's sad, neglected and woeful condition. But, of course, we are in a modern and materialistic society where history, heritage and culture appear to count for very little. Perhaps even the locals have become so familiar with this wreck that they eventually ignore it. Wrapped in black plastic sheets with blue tarpaulins to cover where the plastic has failed the old house has been abandoned and deserted, it's land stripped away many years before and swallowed up by a mass of housing of no architectural merit. What an indignity! To most people it was written off and its number was up. The poor building was riddled with woodworm, death watch beetle, dry rot and wet rot and in fact every known malady - you stood a better chance of getting soaked to the skin inside the building than if you stood in the overgrown gardens in a downpour! If the sun happened to show itself the interior became more akin to the Amazon jungle. Both gardens and building were a dumping ground for all manner of domestic rubbish whilst young trees and ivy had invaded to such an extent that one wall appeared to be held together simply by a thick network of vegetation! It was such a sad sight for what was once a highly important building that had been constructed over 400 years ago and was most probably home to a high ranking officer in Cromwell's Army. It seems such a short time since the wood fire would have burned in the grate of the massive fireplace and kettles sung on the hob whilst parents and children talked and chattered over the day's events.

As I disconsolately left the leaking and decaying hulk in the old Roman town of Godmanchester the clouds began to break and I drove back to Peterborough under bright and crisp skies a very thoughtful person.

But God hadn't finished yet! We hadn't finished yet either - and the Building Preservation Trust, restorers of last resort, were in their element! Tudor Farm escaped unscathed through many a Guy Fawkes night whilst members of our Trust carried out their fire watch; one night it almost succumbed when young arsonists decided the 'call had come from on high' - but not quite!

By some miracle the building clung to life although one wing was mortally wounded in the blaze.

Five years later Tudor Farm has been restored to it's former glory against all odds. Today, 12 years on since I first visited the building, it stands as testimony to that spirit of determination and perseverance (and a modicum of luck) which shone through in bringing this important part of our heritage back from the brink.

Now God IS in his element!

Footnote: Many thanks to Martin England of Warboys who provided me with the details of the windswept pub at sea level in Tick Fen.

DOUGHNUTS AND DAFFODILS

The small town I visited recently displays a gentle mix of stone, brick and burnt orange pantiles vying with patina rich stone roofing slates across a vast array of unsung buildings. It is a joy to behold. But the town in question hides its history very well. It's inhabitants and occasional visitors go quietly but purposefully about their duties be it business or shopping. To all intents and purposes this backwater, in a county not renowned for it's stunning landscapes and scenery but rather it's potatoes and cauliflowers, will continue to sleep as it appears to have done for centuries past.

Having queued for sometime to collect half a dozen of arguably the best jam doughnuts in the business I lazily walk back through the streets gazing at market traders calling their wares under brightly coloured awnings in front of the old town hall. My eyes are drawn to a poster displayed prominently on a wall - the word Hereward is written large not just once but several times and it seems so popular that it is connected with schools, leisure complexes and even health centres. This is Bourne and we are in Hereward Country!

Tourism marketing these days latches onto any likely historic connections with personalities and events which could prove to be both an eye catching symbol and, of course, a big money spinner. Not that far away across the county border a former county town, for it is now shorn of it's old administrative status, had links with the Lord Protector, Oliver Cromwell and used these connections to full advantage. The old town and surrounding countryside is now marketed as Cromwell Country with an appropriate emblem to remind tourists and local inhabitants of it's distinctive and glorious past. Who will be the next personality at the centre of tourism marketing? Could it be 'Haig Country', 'Thatcher Country', 'Blair Country' or even 'Ashdown Country'?

But back to Hereward Country and the small town that produces such delicious doughnuts. It is often described as the coldest place in the Fens but could it really be colder than the days I spent in the Fen Washes at Guyhirn, Whaplode, Denver or Outwell when it seemed there was nothing to stop the biting wind that endlessly swept in from the east. But maybe the locals are right. A few miles down the road an old colleague of mine who recently purchased a fine manor house told of the intense cold he had experienced when the wind blew from the east with nothing to stop it for some 15-20 miles - save for a few tulip and daffodil fields clustered around a town which stood between my friend and the North Sea! It had been he who had introduced me to the doughnuts and a mug of steaming tea as the only known antidote to the penetrating cold. The old 'doughnut' town, now looking rather frayed and shabby at the edges and suffering the sane afflictions of 'anonymous boxes' as many places up and down the land, has earned a fair slice of impressive history. The Romans were most industrious and left in their wake remains of their villages, roads and even a waterway frequently, and probably quite erroneously, described as a canal. It is more likely that Car Dyke, as it is known, was their little way of telling their hostile and belligerent neighbours - that's our fence and don't touch it! William Cecil, the 1st. Lord Burghley and Lord Treasurer to Queen Elizabeth I was born in the town whilst one local family were totally disgraced when they became involved in the Gunpowder Plot no less!

But perhaps the town's most famous son was Hereward the Wake - offspring, it is said, of Lady Godiva and Earl Leofric - who, as a rebel and professional soldier fought for the rights of the Fenmen against the invading Normans and in particular William the Conqueror. Arrogant, unorthodox and highly intelligent he proved to be the only one wise enough to out think and outwit the invaders. His heroic deeds at Ely must rate has his 'finest hour' although it must be admitted he did have an advantage - local knowledge of treacherous ground and the services of a bedraggled old witch that together sent hundreds of Norman soldiers to their death amongst the burning reeds of the fen marshes. Aldreth, Sutton in the Isle and Stretham - the scene of some of the bloodiest battles in the history of the fens - lie silent and peaceful whilst Ely retains it's untroubled yet wily vigilance as it stands proudly above mile upon mile of fenland. In winter the cathedral at Ely is often only visible, like a ghost rising out of the mists of the damp dank land.

Although often inhospitable and desolate at the heart of an 'arctic' winter, tulip time in the fens can only be the opposite. A time of carnival, fiesta and spring madness when the town of Spalding, perched perilously in the middle of nowhere, welcomes everyone from far and wide to join in their celebrations - an annual 'knees up' when something in the order of quarter of a million people pass through the streets to admire and gaze on the floats and flowers of the Tulip Festival. Such an influx does have it's downside as I remember only too well as a child - the everlasting processions and queues of coaches struggling through our city on the way to the tulip fields - and even then they still had some 20 miles to go! For miles around the town, and some claim as far afield as the 'doughnut town', it is a kaleidoscope of colour - not just tulips but hyacinths, narcissi and daffodils spread as far as the eye can see! The 'sea' of colour is but short lived as the heads are cut to adorn the many floats for the day of the parade. Many come, admire and leave believing that the association of tulips with the town is a recent happening - but they would be wrong. The tulip was introduced over 400 years ago and ever since that time Spalding has had links with the Dutch, but not always peaceful - particularly when they turned up to drain the fens! The festival grew almost as an afterthought from someone's realisation that the heads cut from the plants and dumped unceremoniously by the roadside could be used to good effect. Ever since that day some 40 years ago the little town has hosted the largest event of it's kind in the world.

The town is easily forgotten under the heaving masses of humanity searching and stretching to ensure they see the best of the blooms and the parade floats. Truthfully, Spalding is much like any other fen town with vast unforbidding and unending spaces where sky and landscape seem to be permanently one. Extracting myself from the melee I head out west to the very fringes of the fens in search of peaceful countryside and flower decked winding byways and respite from that cutting wind.

I'll take the doughnuts but you can keep the daffodils (and tulips)!

AND IS THERE HONEY STILL FOR TEA?

Travelling the B1040 road between what were once two of the most ambitious, astute and wealthy Fenland abbeys is more akin to crossing a bleak, windswept bridge between two totally different landscapes - the Lincolnshire and Cambridgeshire fens with the all pervading sprawl of the nearby city of Peterborough and it's once fabulously rich monastery of Medehamstede or Golden Borough standing guard in the distance. The journey some 800 or 900 years ago could not have been that much different although no doubt the landscape would have been more wooded and the many dykes, rivers and marshes generously stocked with all manner of wildfowl and fish - a poacher's paradise! Today the 'eyes' or 'isles' with their abbey churches still stand sentinel as in days gone by - a marker and guide to the weary traveller.

The abbey dedicated to St.Bartholomew but truly in memory of the founder St.Guthlac, a monk from Yorkshire who had arrived some 1300 years ago along with his boatman Tatwin, suffered from every known catastrophe. Raids by Danish invaders, several fires and even an earthquake in 1118 still did not quell its desire to survive. Disaster not only struck the abbey church but the whole town. The old gentlemen sitting beside the unique triangular bridge will spin you yarns of all manner of misfortunes, the fateful floods of 1947 being amongst the worst. In that year the town's streets became waterways and the 'danger bell' in the abbey was heard for the first time since 1880 - many believe these horrific scenes will be repeated but with even greater losses. The triangular or Trinity Bridge as it is often called, could also tell a tale. Many kings and commoners have arrived and departed from here, most notably Henry VI who arrived on one of the waterways that once passed under its arches and stayed in the town for 3 nights. Otherwise this curious structure, more akin to a signal box and station that has lost its railway, continues the long tradition of being the seat of the 'local parliament'.

But all this cannot compare with the 'miracle' that took place within the walls of the abbey concerning a certain Earl Waltheof. Although a benefactor and re-builder of the abbey he became greedy and having incurred the wrath of the king no less he was duly executed and buried with great dignity. To the great consternation of the ecclesiastical hierarchy pilgrims began to visit his tomb in the abbey in increasing numbers so much so that the tomb was ordered to be opened. The contents, some 15 years after the Earl's unfortunate and untimely demise, stunned the clergy - the body was untouched and showed no signs of decay. Even more amazingly the head had been re-united with its body with only but a small red mark to show the sign of the executioner's strike! The abbot never fully recovered from the events and continued to have visions of the 're-united Earl' for many years until his own death. How could anyone say that the town is boring and mundane with such a story as this?

On a warm mid summer evening in the shadows of the ruined abbey you can feel completely at peace with the world as bees hum and buzz on their endless travels between the masses of wildflowers set amidst the tall waving grass and the ancient stone walls - no doubt their home for far longer than we can imagine. It's almost as if the abbey's past has crept up and caressed you into a soothing and compelling dream of when monks went about their saintly duties in glorious orchard and walled garden. There is always something new to absorb and delight in over this most historic and fascinating isle of the fens despite the modern day "vandalism" inflicted upon its fragile setting. Crowland is now a place you rarely pass through even on the way to somewhere else since it now sports a brand new bypass that has offered up opportunities for money grabbing developers to fill in the luscious green meadows, almost up to the abbey itself, with unsophisticated and lifeless brick boxes. Once you could look back on the town and see the abbey silhouetted in it's sylvan setting against a golden sun sinking across the nothingness of the fens. As you leave now, crossing the acres of tarmac that have invaded the once rich meadowland, there is still a fine view of the abbey surrounded by trees on it's miniature island; it survives and remains a haven of mystery and antiquity, but it's just not the same!

I turn my back and head due south across the open wastes of Morris Fen and Old Pepper Lake, reliving memories of the heroic deeds of Vermuyden and his fellow pioneers, passing Singlesole and Singlecote Farms and the ancient watercourse known as Cat's

Water which must have seen activity in Prehistoric and Roman times. Just in sight, like minute eruptions on a well ironed landscape, are Buke Horn Toll and Powder Blue Farms with their fully grown shelter of alders and poplars, leaning, as if in unison, from the south westerlies and pointing to the sky like a giant network of witches brooms. Powder Blue must strike anyone as an unusual name to give to a fenland farm but so much past lies buried here with few realising it. Like French Farm and French Drove they are reminders of the Huguenots who 300 years ago set up woad or 'poudre bleu' industries for the then very successful clothing trade. There are many more intriguing names in the fens - Teakettle Hall, Botany Bay, Rogues Alley, Hollow Heap and Whipchicken Farm - all founded on incidents lost in the mists of time. Some are even more obscure than these!

But my sights are set on a more substantial island rising ahead of me as if in friendly greeting to a long lost and weary traveller. However my attention is strangely drawn away from my goal to an ancient timber framed farmhouse set below the level of the road and close to an arrow straight fenland 'cut'. A grubby sign informs me that this 'heap' is For Sale but I wonder what there is left to sell! Surely there can be nothing? As I mulled over the indignity this building had suffered a wizened old man appeared standing in the opening of the adjoining black tarred and weather boarded barn holding, what at first sight, seemed to be a shotgun. My day dreaming suddenly ended and I racked my thoughts as to how I could stall what might be an awkward situation and speed my passage into the town for a well earned pot of Earl Grey tea with cream and strawberry jam scones at the Abbey Tearooms.

'Ive just been thinking'. That was a good start, I thought. But no such luck with a stubborn old Fenman!

With no sign of a breakthrough I tried to change the conversation, what little there was.

'Are the tearooms open in the town?'

'Loik as they are but I n'er set foot in 'em'

'Why's that?' I enquired, ever hopeful that this might prove a useful release from my difficult predicament.

'Loik as o'ive git my own 'wittals'

'Oh so you grow your own vegetables then?'

'No. Course not - bees do gud enough job fur me'.

Suddenly the penny dropped. He had hives that supplied him with more than enough honey.

'What about strawberries then?' I asked, thinking laterally around cream and strawberry jam scones.

'Course, you silly 'ul davil - them's moin at the tearooms!'

Sitting down in his cosy living room, which bore little or no resemblance to the state of the building outside, we talked of fen life and the characters which make this land such a rich tapestry, whilst consuming piping hot scones laden with cream and strawberry jam. Why bother to call at the tearooms when I could enjoy the fruits of the fens at first hand and in good company? I never did ask his name and knowing fen folk he would more as like not tell me. But what on earth was the gun for?

Guns bring back memories of when we used to cycle from the city some 5 or 6 miles into the country to pick as many blackberries as possible to accompany apples in delicious pies and crumbles. The fields, I remember, were located just below an enormous television mast that beamed out programmes far and wide. To this day I still don't know who the farmer was, and I'm quite sure I want to remain ignorant of his identity, as the peaceful pastime of gathering the 'fruits of the fields' was rudely interrupted by his ominous booming voice. It took us only one sight of what seemed to be a shotgun under his arm for us to gather our baskets and head off as far away as possible! The great pity was that his land and hedgerows, if they were really his, grew the most amazing, juicy blackberries as our hands showed testimony to. Many a time as late summer approached we were often tempted to climb the gate again - just for the taste of a few berries!

I gathered myself and my thoughts together and heaping profuse thanks upon my host for his hospitality and generous gifts I headed off up the slight rise over the site of the old railway line and into the Isle of Thorns just as the sun, now a deep golden orange ball, was sleepily sinking in the west casting deep shadows across the magical remains of yet another abbey. The ancient stones that have witnessed many a sad and happy event almost glow with warmth and life in the dying embers of the day. Many say the small town doesn't give the appearance of being inhospitable, cold and dreary unlike many of its neighbours. It pervades a quiet air of orderliness, permanency and almost aloofness - certainly not all fen like. Perhaps the often quoted old rhyme about Fenland Abbeys was closest to the mark when it described the 'isle' as 'the flower of many a fair tree'. That the monks here vinified their own wine from capacious vineyards and enjoyed bounteous harvests from far spreading orchards and bowers must speak volumes for this well favoured and protected little haven. In the heyday of the monasteries the local monks were the envy of their brethren in many of the nearby abbeys including that of Medehamstede renowned to be the wealthiest by virtue of its title Golden Borough. Alas the grandeur was short lived and Thorney Abbey is now but a remnant of what was built to the glory of God. Yet the little town and it's abbey church have settled down into a peaceful, unhurried and contented existence no doubt basking in the glories and riches that have been. All is calm apart from the noise of the trunk road which dissects the town but which will shortly become a backwater once the by pass is complete.

The Abbey bell soothingly reminds me that I have to travel on. Passing the Abbey Tearooms, now closed for the day, I notice a menu hanging forlornly in the window - surprisingly strawberry jam and cream teas are at the head of the list! Another well penned and brightly coloured poster stares out at passers-by announcing 'Local Honey For Sale'. My mind races back to that tea I had not long consumed in the old farmhouse.

Would there be honey still for tea?

Of course - I had a years supply in my rucksack!

Footnote: The village and abbey of Thorney has now been bypassed {2006}.

TOWN AND COUNTRY

Many over the centuries including none other than the famous traveller and writer Celia Fiennes have admired this town set splendidly on the banks of the River Welland. It matters little whether you view the town from afar over water meadow or from the river bridge, a fine edifice constructed in 1849 with its 'Tudor style' houses on the north bank. The end result is always the same - perfection. Little if anything is out of place, almost as if it had been set out by some divine hand. Few towns or cities can boast such wonderful individual buildings and delightful townscape that brings endless pleasure to the promenader.

Its royal connections are impressive and unsurpassed. At least 16 reigning monarchs accompanied by an unknown number of royal relatives have visited and enjoyed the visual and gastronomic delights just as the many tourists and locals do today. Throughout it's long and often turbulent history it has never lacked for wont of colourful fairs, feasts and markets complimented by fine alehouses, inns and eating houses. No wonder the town was host to the largest man known, Daniel Lambert - he must have been spoilt for choice!

It is a pleasure and something of a rarity these days to be able to browse and shop in relative peace whilst calling at the market stalls with their brightly coloured awnings in Red Lion Square in the shadow of the soaring steeple of All Saint's Church. Spare a moment or two and enter the cool peacefulness of this church, one of Stamford's most ancient and seek out the many brasses dedicated to the omnipresent Brownes. Once described as 'merchants of very wonderful riches' they founded one of the many medieval hospitals in the town built appropriately just after the Lancastrians had had a field day sacking and burning everything to the ground. In the Middle Ages the town hosted a substantial university and 17 churches - miraculously almost half of the churches survive today.

I have mixed emotions and memories of the town. When as a child of five I was unceremoniously hauled kicking and screaming into the local hospital for tonsil removal it was made abundantly clear that egg sandwiches were essential for my survival and well being but that I could have endless quantities of ice cream - when it was all over, of course! Egg sandwiches are etched in my mind forever and surprisingly they have never passed my lips since! But not all memories are quite so bad.

Picnics to the 'hills and holes' on the outskirts of the town were something totally different. I sometimes wonder now what on earth those medieval quarry masters and stonemasons would have thought of us running up and down, playing tag and even eating cheese, not egg, sandwiches and raspberry jelly on the very site of their hard labours - what sacrilege! That this 'playground' had been the largest source of 'freestone' in East Anglia during medieval times which built many a cathedral, church and collegiate complex across the country did not even enter our heads. A little wiser in my teens I regularly cycled past the quarries - now a haven for all manner of wildlife, but still the scene of many family picnics - and stopped off to admire the village church, an Anglo Saxon masterpiece of national importance, and delight in the groups of cottages which displayed an amazing yet harmonious array of styles, shapes and sizes. As a student I expanded my horizons a little further spending time soaking up the atmosphere and delights of Barnack '- as fine a town all of stone as may be seen'- before returning to the Millstone pub just round the corner from the 'hills and holes' for a quick half and a ploughmans in the convivial surroundings of this most ancient of hostelries.

This is Clare Country.

Often described as the 'peasant poet', quite wrongly, Clare was born just down the road in a village which is at the very heart of the land that he loved and eulogised over in his poetry. He may well have even visited and pondered over the 'hills and holes' and written verse to encapsulate the depth of history and feeling lying in the soil. Always regarded as a Northamptonshire poet it would be difficult to imagine his reaction to find that the village of his birth, Helpston, is now in Cambridgeshire. He was not a Fen poet either, in truth, but rather one of the low heaths, commons and woodlands that abounded around his home and which covered a rich past - the centre of one of the largest concentrations of Roman occupation in the kingdom. He lived and wrote in an age of discovery and overwhelming desire to understand the ancient civilisations when country squires and earls fell over themselves to promote and support investigations whether it be of the local Roman fort or some grand complex of the pharaohs in Egypt. It was an exciting time, both underground and over ground, for such a gifted intelligent man who, we can see today, had more than a touch of genius.

As the River Nene meanders on it's peaceful and lugubrious way through water meadow, mill pond and sweet, luscious woodland to it's destiny with the sea it traverses fine and delicate landscapes so well known to Clare. He would have walked this countryside many times, his keen eye taking in and noting the gentle pastoral landscape of the riverside, the flower bedecked heath land and the cottages, farmhouses and churches that made up hamlet and village alike - Southey Wood and Lady Wood, Sutton Heath and the Hanglands, Walcot Hall and Pellet Hall and Woodcroft Castle - all were his 'country'. His was a 'country' of times when he could spend a few hours lazily wandering down richly endowed hedgerowed lanes with butterflies flitting from plant to plant and a chorus of birds telling the world how good life was whilst the carpet of wildflowers bowed their heads in the rich pasture. The search for the soaring skylark and its haunting call was commonplace as was the straining to reach fat and tasty blackberries clustered on the very highest and thorniest of briars. In the distance the bell tolls from the ancient church steeple as it has done for centuries past calling the faithful few to prayer and reminding us all of the important feeling of 'belonging'. The fruit is gathered in and disgorged onto the old kitchen table. The best are selected for bottling into row upon row of kilner jars whilst the remainder are picked at by eager children before being whisked away to the cool whitewashed pantry ready for making into some magnificent cooking bonanza later in the day.

Clare would be angry and mystified at what we have perpetrated on the precious countryside he knew and loved as child and man. As the clock on Clare's old parish church, beneath which he lies buried, reaches mid day his own lines come flooding back –

'the mid day hour of twelve the clock counts 'oer…………

A sultry stillness lulls the air asleep……………………

{John Clare 1793 – 1864}

His village sleeps

This was true countryside.

The Butter Cross and War Memorial, Market Square, Whittlesey

By Moreton's Leam in the Nene Washes, Eldernell

The Five Chimneys, latterly the White Swan pub at Sea Level, Tick Fen, Warboys

The Baptist Chapel, Warboys

Old brick bridge, dated 1833, over Thorney River, Murrow

Browne's Hospital, Stamford

Derelict Tudor Farm, Earning Street, Godmanchester

Restored and lived in Tudor Farm, Earning Street, Godmanchester

The West Front, Crowland Abbey

The Triangular Bridge, Crowland

Old Cottage by Thorney River, Thorney

Fen subsidence - Gothic House Farm, French Drove, North Fen amidst flax

Distant view of Stamford and it's churches from the west

The Clare Memorial,
Helpston

Helpston Church
and
John Clare's grave

*Southey Wood
near Helpston
in Clare Country*

*St. Vincent's Cross,
Nene Terrace looking to
Singlesole and Morris Fen*

Thorney River, Murrow looking towards Parson Drove

IV

TIME
TO TRAVEL

SEASIDE SORCERY

I may be an old romantic in an age of rapidly shrinking lines of communication and mind bogglingly fast economic development but what has happened to the once proud British seaside resort and it's much heralded unique brand of architecture? Even the famous, or some would say the infamous seaside landlady has become an early victim.

Many a resort, once alive with hoards of holidaymakers, young and old, and boasting regular appearances at delightful theatres by nationally known performers supported by the classic chorus girls, has lost it's vitality and claim to being the pride and glory of all 'watering holes'. Seaside pier and winter garden pavilions have all seen better days - the pier theatre, miniature train and chamber orchestra, so synonymous with resorts, have all succumbed. Glorious floral bandstands in finely tended parks are a shadow of their illustrious past with few now fulfilling their original purpose. Gone with them are the rows of brightly coloured deckchairs and their occupants, so very much at peace with themselves relaxing in warm summer sunshine.

Weston - Super - Mare on the Somerset coast was the scene of many a happy holiday in the 50's for my sister and I - luckily our grandparents lived but a very short distance from the beach and all it's fascinating pleasures – the wonderful donkey rides and Punch and Judy shows. But how this once mighty and revered resort has fallen from it's glorious and thriving past. The entry to the town today is grim and foreboding much as you would expect on approaching any humdrum town in Britain - acres of tarmac to 'feed' the everlasting thirst for the infernal combustion engine, a ubiquitous Sainsbury's supermarket and the obligatory trolleys allocated their own parking lot. An umbilical chord of roads fans out amidst a sea of standardised bungalows and houses that would not look out of place anywhere in the country. The town itself has all but lost it's individuality and unique seaside character only to be replaced by tacky, dirty and tired looking streets and shops with not even the pier retaining it's resplendent glory. It is by no means unusual - Hunstanton, Skegness, Clacton, Llandudno, Barry Island and even the world famous Blackpool have diminished in stature and succumbed to the ever spreading standardisation! Individuality and uniqueness appear to mean nothing in what seems to be a relentless quest for greater and greater wealth.

The day used to be when Weston was 'fed' by an everlasting flow of trains disgorging eager holidaymakers from all over the kingdom on day trips and the long awaited summer holidays - happy to sample the delights of a premier resort. As a young boy I impatiently awaited our arrival for our summer holidays at a flower decked and sparkling station where I would stand in amazement, bucket and spade in hand, watching a continuous flow of chocolate and cream coaches hauled by gleaming engines arriving at the excursion platforms. The hub of activity - trains arriving and leaving, holidaymakers engaging porters to help with mountains of luggage, children standing and staring in wide eyed wonder and a Station Master, with red carnation in button hole, grandly overseeing proceedings - created an air of expectation and excitement. But this has all vanished - so quickly, it seems, that there has been little time to react to the takeover bid by the car. The excursion platforms complete with engine shed, turntable and water tower became deserted almost overnight, overtaken by weeds, decay and vandalism. The main station had most of its tracks ripped up in the drive for rationalisation and modernisation and is now but a remnant of it's former glory. The chocolate and cream station signs that stood on the platform to the height of a man have gone as has the ability of a passenger to ascertain where on earth they are on their journey - standardised concrete British Rail lamp standards with station names set 10 feet in the air in plastic shade are now the order of the day! So much for the modern age! The site of the excursion platforms has now given way after many desolate years to a Tesco supermarket and a bus and coach park - apparently the impressive sea front bus station, a masterpiece of flowery Edwardian design, was found to have outlived it's useful life at the very moment a property company offered vast sums for the re development of the site! This wonderful and evocative monument to transport was flattened without as much as a whimper and a dull, unimaginative multi storey block of flats now stands in its place. Visitors now arriving by coach must walk the enlightening 3/4 mile through depressing streets to an even more dreary and windswept seafront.

The Knightstone Theatre stands purely as a symbol of what was Weston's glorious past and the Knightstone Baths grow decrepit and aged with neglect whilst the authorities haggle with some entrepreneur over what the rotting shell is worth. The main pier stands majestically at the centre of the front as if in defiance of even worse atrocities yet to be perpetrated - shorn already of it's theatre and now bestowed with a fruit machine and bingo palace it's pride has been shattered and destroyed without trace. What of Birnbeck Pier at the very limits of the front? It now stands like some rusting hulk of a steel dinosaur, unloved and uncared for and rapidly falling bit by bit into the Bristol Channel. No one seems to care anymore! The fish and chips, candyfloss and shellfish stalls have lost their magic as have the funfairs and the pitch and putt - they all look faded and tatty around the edges. Where have those gentlemen with handkerchiefs or newspapers on their heads gone and how we miss the scrumptious and fruity Lyons Maid orange lollies from the vendor with his pedal powered cart. Modern day ice creams and lollies just cannot compete and even sand in the sandwiches doesn't seem the same! Yet the donkey rides on the beach seem timeless – little children still queue with parents, grandparents and friends, so keen to have a ride on these gentle creatures that all have names. Just like domestic pets they lap up affection from the tourists. Thank god this is one of the few seaside pleasures that has not changed – and at Weston super Mare they have been part of the seaside scenery with the same family owners for over 100 years!

Travelling to seaside resorts by steam train was a magical mystery tour in itself traversing town and city and the rural backwaters with myriad scenery and a gloriously compelling mix of styles at stations and halts on the way. Reminders of where you were heading or where you had just come from stared down at you from the watercolour prints framed above your carriage seat. Even steam engines and their drivers had their own personality depending upon where you travelled in the country. Some still yearn for a return to a semblance of what these famous resorts once were and restoration of the civic pride which was their hallmark even after the high days of the Victorian era had vanished and they relied almost entirely on the intrepid day tripper.

Nostalgia this all may be but how good it would be to see some seaside sorcery again!

Footnote:

During a visit to Weston super Mare in August 2006 I was mortified to witness the rapid decay to the town and it's sea front. The Knightstone Baths were no more with the steelwork of new flats rising from the ashes whilst the Knightstone Theatre stood as an empty shell no doubt awaiting the demolition gangs. The town and it's streets were unkempt whilst the 'rag tag' of 'could be anywhere' shops, stores and houses depressed me; there seems to be little 'spirit of place' or pride left and sadly few notice or care that it is happening under their very noses.

At least the donkey rides are still there and giving endless pleasure to children.

SPREADING THE WORD

One of my favourite pastimes as a teenager was to cycle at leisure around town and countryside enjoying and photographing humble cottages and ancient parish churches. In those days there was little danger from grid locked roads, speeding cars, thundering juggernauts and overpowering pollution although even then we felt highways and byways were far too busy and a threat to human and animal life. It bears little comparison with today's mayhem and suffocating poisons we have to suffer. In the early 60's the very first motorways had only just been opened for business and the country had not yet started on it's explosion in car ownership. Some 35 years or so on and the road system around my old home city of Peterborough once a peaceful and sleepy place, is more akin to Spaghetti Junction or even Chicago!

To my great pleasure many of my cycling ventures were extended into totally uncharted territory during the school holidays thanks to British Rail. One summer visit to Clacton on Sea offered me the opportunity to plan tours around the splendid Essex villages and their churches - a far better prospect than being anchored to a beach!

Many Essex churches are renowned for their impressive brick towers, often timbered and thatched porches and frequent location at the centre of an ancient village community grouped around a green upon which life has been played out for centuries. One village, Great

Bentley, has a green so vast that it is difficult to see the cottages on the opposite side; it is in fact the largest village green in the county and some would go as far as to say it was bordering upon being a common. No doubt village folk recall the young children dancing round the maypole and retired gentlemen leaning on their sticks and sipping a pint whilst Morris men played out age old traditions to ancient tunes in front of the village inn. The cricket team, in their dazzling 'whites' lazily went through their ritual as a few sleepy spectators, straw hats propped delicately on bronzed heads, reclined in deckchairs and sagely considered the merits of a missed catch. The pace was nothing but slow but why should they bother as there was no strict timetable - plenty of time for another pint or two!

In my travels I discovered that churches could occasionally be found well away from a village centre almost as if they had parted company from their intended community as a result of some catastrophic event. I remember quite vividly entering the cool whitewashed interior of one such well secluded church through a massive ancient door complete with key almost a foot long. My eye was inexorably drawn to an amazing series of wall paintings strategically placed close to the 13th.century chancel arch. I was not prepared for what I saw - vivid portrayals of Doom and Hell and the particularly nasty consequences of what might befall those who did not keep to the straight and narrow. There can be little doubt as to the success of displaying the scriptures in pictures thus to a populace that lacked in reading skills - it had me transfixed!

As a young lad I can recall with admiration and awe the majestic sight of our Fenland village parish church and it's impressive broach spire soaring up to the sky where a rag tag of crows noisily argued with each other around the weathervane - no doubt this 'crow court' was deciding what were to be the day's pressing issues. It held the same ethereal magic on a balmy Summer evening or crisp Winter afternoon – the sun, a massive golden ball sunk rapidly in the sky silhouetting the church against the Fenland landscape and creating a cascade of myriad lights in the stained glass windows. On a far smaller scale, but at the centre of our family for generations, was the diminutive Methodist Chapel in the High Street where a small and only too often ageing congregation still meet every Sunday to continue their ritualistic gathering. The little building started life in the nearby hamlet of Little Raveley but was dismantled and moved brick by brick to our village where it was lovingly and enthusiastically re erected. It became and has thus remained the focus of many a village event and the centre for regular services which seemed to attract some of the most idiosyncratic and amusing local preachers. One in particular frequently kept the younger members of the congregation in fits of hysterical laughter. During the course of his 'fire and brimstone' sermons his false teeth were often projected at great velocity from the pulpit to land at the feet of one of the giggling boys and girls. With heads buried in their knees they tried desperately to stifle their laughter in case parents should notice and remove them swiftly for chastisement off the premises.

Being a local preacher could not have been easy and even more so in such far flung and isolated communities. My grandfather, a Fenman born over some 100 years ago, had become a local preacher ' on trial' in 1909 and spent over 50 years touring the small fenland villages in all weathers to 'spread the word'. Apart from preaching at our local chapel, which, of course was but a few steps from Lodge House on the opposite side of the High Street, he cycled to outlying communities in the depth of the fens. Aided only by a carbide lamp, which were notoriously erratic and unreliable, it must have been a sheer miracle that he managed to reach his destination, preach the message to the faithful few and return home in one piece! No doubt he had some narrow escapes on those dark fen roads bordered by deep, evil smelling dykes. His mobility was eventually updated by the acquisition of a moped, once cycling had become more than he could cope with. But according to my father he still quite frequently arrived back from his preaching appointments covered from head to toe in white hoar frost and his clothes as stiff as a board. Few today could ever contemplate the hardship, grit and determination it must have required for these unsung rural preachers to go about their duties. The onset of spring and summer must have been something of a welcome relief to my grandfather and even something of a pleasure for him to be passing through village, farmyard and field with warming sunshine on his back and nature at it's very best.

Today it is still a pleasure to leisurely walk through a country churchyard, pass under the arched roof of the lychgate which has seen so many sad and happy events over the years and enter the ice cool quiet of the ancient church to muse upon it's long traditional role in the spiritual life of the community. Considering everything and taking my thoughts to a practical conclusion perhaps there is no real need for either church or chapel - that is, the building. John Wesley who spread the word at street corner, on the village green and often from horseback had no particular need for a building that is, until his peculiar brand of Protestantism took off and supporters decided to erect buildings for the purpose of spreading the word. It must be admitted the loss of Church and Chapel to town and village landscape would be immense and immeasurable and would create a large void in the traditional village scene. On reflection most of our nation no longer see any need for spiritual support and guidance, the 'rich' church and it's hierarchy being looked on as 'out of date', 'not in touch' and 'irrelevant' to today's lifestyle. There is no doubt that the churches and chapels of past days stand testament to the faith and spirit of their communities. But perhaps we should rather consider returning our churches to their first and intended use - a 'market place' where the community met, bought and sold their goods be it vegetables, fruit, garments, eggs, chickens, pigs and sheep and permit services of worship to take a sharing role instead of the present dominant one.

This community based Church proposal recently became a possibility in our own village of Llanfynydd when the impending loss of the Post Office, a lifeline for many of the older residents, led me to ask the vicar if this 'service' could be housed temporarily in the North Vestry of the Parish Church or even in the tower. Sadly, although he was supportive, his Parochial Church Council did not see the proposition this way rejecting the scheme out of hand as being totally unsuitable for a church. One aged Welsh member even suggested that the vicar and I were attempting to bring ungodly acts into the House of God apparently comparing a community Post Office with the money lenders in the temple! Maybe the time has come for society to turn full circle, as has happened many a time throughout history, and 'look inward' once more to the community and set aside the 'I'm alright Jack' attitude that has come to prevail in this country. At least the churches and chapels would be used and become a central player in creating an identity and meaning to the community far in excess of what has been apparent in the best part of the 20th. Century. I cannot see the 21st. century being any different. Until the coming of iron, coal and steel life, essentially rural, revolved around the farming calendar, the church and it's incumbent, the seasons and of course the Saints Days. Even the moving of cattle from summer to winter pasture and their return centred on Saints Days. Sadly transhumance has all but ceased and in the few places in Snowdonia where it is still practised there is now no need for the Hafoty and Hendref, the summer and winter dwellings, to which the herdsman and his family made their annual pilgrimage. Often no more than a single roomed hovel it was seen off rapidly by the car. Daily demands of rural folk were minimal; they sought successful crops and livestock and regarded the Church as a means of support in their endeavours on the land and in their spiritual requirements through good and lean times.

The arrival of the Non Conformist preachers spitting 'fire and brimstone' and pouring out threats of doom on those who did not repent came at a time of flagging fortunes in the moral and spiritual well being of the country. The Welsh certainly took to this new religious fervour with vigour, chapels becoming a total way of life for 6 days a week and the bastion of the community spirit.

But all this goodwill and spirit has evaporated with churches and chapels closing and becoming redundant every day of the week that passes. Genuine attempts to create an active life for these crucially important elements in our culture and ever changing landscape are frequently met by cries of reaction and horror especially from the dwindling band of churchgoers. What can be wrong with using a church to serve the community in every sense of the word and allow it to earn it's living? Heaven knows I have been harangued enough times by parish church members complaining bitterly that their church is poor and they can't afford to maintain the crumbling, ancient fabric.

Perhaps congregations, priests and ministers should be reminded of a quotation from the Bible -

'Where two or three are gathered together' -field, car, pub, home or office - 'there I shall be also'.

GOD HASN'T TURNED UP THE HEAT – YET!!

BABY IT'S COLD OUTSIDE

It's 6.30 in the morning and it almost feels that we are 'practising' for the lambing that starts in earnest in two weeks time. Peering through the bedroom curtain my eyes fall upon that dreaded 'white stuff' as far as one can see. It may create wonderful artistic patterns on the branches of the trees and hedges as have never been seen before but to the shepherd it's certainly not welcome! If the snowfall has been as heavy as feared from first sightings then Wales will almost certainly close up the shutters. Lulled into a false sense of security by winter after winter of unseasonably mild weather it's hard to remember that we are still in February and at the mercy of what we all know is a fickle climate. Setting aside the vagaries of global warming we all know how unpredictable the British weather can be.

As a teenager at grammar school winters always seemed far more severe and prolonged than they are now as we enter the early years of the 21st.century. One master who taught me French and, of course, drove either a dilapidated Renault or Citroen 2CV, always gave the appearance, whatever the weather, that he was frozen to the marrow. I was never quite sure why but probably wrongly assumed it was on account that he had once resided in one of the warmer parts of France and was not accustomed to our often bitter winters.

My apparent 'love affair' with severe climatic aberrations followed me after school when I left for Leicester to train as an architect. The heady days of the late 60's and early 70's offered up some of the most foul and loathsome weather imaginable - almost always when I was planning to spend a weekend at home to regain lost ground on food consumption. The God's were certainly against me and, I suppose, many of my student friends. How could anyone forget the nightmare train journey one bitter November afternoon that started at Leicester London Road Station and which should have ended in Norwich. As students I'm sure we took the events in our stride making light of the conditions that we suffered - from the time we stepped into the coaches that appeared to be leaking and hissing steam from every joint and orifice until the time came for British Rail, or rather the driver, to decide enough was enough and the train would go no further! Wrapped together with copious lengths of scarves we squeezed ourselves into a compartment for the journey to Hell. Not content with what seemed to be a lethargic engine (or driver) we were stopped every few miles as frozen points and signal wires were manhandled and cajoled to allow us once more to resume our passage. I had visions at one point that our painful progress would lead to one ultimate decision - to abandon the train miles from any civilisation! So isolated did we feel in our steam laden compartment that we might as well have been the only train running on BR - it certainly felt like it! How close we were to the truth! After waiting for almost an hour in the dead of the Leicestershire countryside whilst the driver and fireman helped a crossing keeper defrost the gates that had frozen in position across the tracks, one of our colleagues decided he could hold out no longer and the call of nature won. Sliding open the compartment door he bravely placed a foot in the steam laden corridor only for him to let out a shriek of horror as he slid to the floor on a sheet of ice and skated freely down to the toilet at the end of the coach! He returned a little while later only to reach the compartment door at the very moment the train lurched forward from it's enforced halt - he was once more catapulted forward and became prostrate on the 'iced' floor once again! The moral of our friend's little adventure has to be that if you must visit the 'little room' on the train then take crampons and an ice axe!

Squeaking and rattling the train wended it's way onward. We had become so paranoid as to the eventual outcome of the journey that we willed the train to tarry as short a time as possible at each of the stations in fear that it would itself freeze to the tracks. Some 6 hours later and 4 hours behind schedule recognizable landmarks peered out of the night under the eerie glow of marshalling yard lights - I had reached my destination! But there was to be a nasty sting in the tail before I could feel fully confident of stepping onto the terra firma of the station platform. Pulling to a juddering halt it suddenly became clear that every door on the train had become frozen - we must have appeared like the inmates of a prison to the platform staff as they bent their minds round an almighty problem. Then from the gloomy depths of the station an old porter emerged waving a lump of iron in the air - panic spread through the ranks of the students and the other passengers. Was this some maniac or a porter who could no longer stand the strain and had gone off his trolley? As if from nowhere others followed and began to lay about the doors of the coaches like devils possessed. Freedom was rapidly granted by the crowbar bearers and we stood relieved on the station platform. Needless to say the train went no further that night and I cannot say I blamed it - lady luck might just have run out!

Looking back on the events I can only have admiration for the grit and determination of the staff who ensured that our train got through. Today, attitudes don't bear comparison - the slightest hint of adverse weather and the country grinds to a halt despite the modern technology we boast about. It little seems to matter what time of year it is - disruption is assured on account of the wrong type of leaves, a strange and hitherto unknown consistency of snow and inconsiderate wind speeds! We must be turning into a nation of 'softies' unable to withstand the rigours of a normal British winter.

During the winters at grammar school I, along with several others, were given the task of producing and editing the School Magazine - an exemplary piece of literary skill. We invariably attached nicknames to many of the masters no doubt just as schoolboys do today - Nobby the Art Master, Mole the Music Teacher, Spud the English Master and, of course Buddha the Headmaster! All of these vividly descriptive titles were displayed for everyone to read, including the teaching staff, in our splendid magazine. The French Master, Charlie, as he was affectionately known, always sporting a checked scarf neatly wrapped and knotted around his neck, drew a great deal of derision and mockery without the taunters fully knowing the reason for his strange dress code come rain, hail and sun. Much to our chagrin he inevitably turned up for our lessons whatever the weather! One of my colleagues on the magazine committee, who had an uncanny knack of plucking apt phrases from nowhere and, was no doubt, destined to become a high flying journalist, produced an absolute gem for dear Charlie that summed up both the teacher and the weather we had to battle through to reach our lessons.

'Baby it's cold outside'.

PLASTIC FANTASTIC

The menu stared out at me across the restaurant where everyone, seated on red plastic covered bench seats at gunmetal grey formica topped tables, appeared to be eating exactly the same meal - sausage, chips and peas! The picture in the illuminated menu looked little different from the fayre turned out on the plates - plastic sausages, plastic chips and plastic peas with the occasional plastic egg all being eaten by 'plastic' people! How boring and unappetising! But in the late 60's what else was on the menu for hard up University students?

Faced with the blandness of a utilitarian Midlands city that had little going for it except perhaps the shady sylvan setting of the Town Hall Square and the bustling excitement of the largest open air market in the country where traders almost came to blows in the frenzy to sell their wares, it was little surprise most students 'slipped into oblivion' propping up the Union bar! The drinks certainly helped to blot out the rhetoric of none other than Jack Straw, the present Foreign Secretary, who exhorted us all to rise up against the Tory oppressors!

My 7 years as a student seemed to be a never ending battle for survival lurching from crisis to crisis in a vain attempt to keep a few pounds in my pocket. Gone are the days when lodgings cost but £5 a week! The plastic sausage, chips and peas were begrudgingly given up to cheese and onion rolls from the sandwich bar just shouting distance from our studios - that is until I was laid low by a bout of salmonella that left me feeling my end had come. Suddenly sausage, chips and peas did not seem that bad after all as I certainly needed something substantial after cycling some 4 or 5 miles every morning from the suburbs into college. How I managed to arrive in one piece must have been a miracle; with 'double elephant' size portfolio strapped to my back I prayed for a calm day otherwise I was the closest design to a land yacht at full speed and imminent lift off!

Our studio was located on one of the upper floors of a converted hosiery warehouse and was renowned to be the biggest fire risk in the city - not surprising when you mix students with a cast iron columned and timber floored building. It became common practice for us to view the girls training to become caterers on the floor below through knot holes in the ancient floorboards and we frequently aimed pencils or anything we could lay our hands on through the holes into the culinary delights below. If they had found their target it surely couldn't have made the dish any worse considering the smells that emanated from the depths!

In an age when plastics and fibreglass had become all important ingredients in design and every day life it was most unfortunate that several students conveniently forgot the 'no smoking' rule with all too disastrous consequences. A rapid exit was made by everyone (including the catering girls) down the only stairs (wooden, of course!) past the shattered 'Break Glass in case of Fire' and into the street amidst a dozen or more fire engines spilling their crews and hoses back up the stairs we had just come down! Fortunately the vast majority of the 'exits' were false alarms since the chance of escaping 'uncooked' were quite low as was soon to be proved only too graphically some two doors up. As if to reinforce our potentially dire situation a hosiery and knitwear warehouse identical to our studios caught fire and was consumed in a matter of a few hours. As students of architecture we were taken along by our materials and technology lecturer to view the mayhem at a safe distance - the outcome for the poor building was total meltdown! Within 6 months the University authorities thought better of risking a similar incident and we were all moved to a 'safer' building sadly without the holes in the floor.

Student Rag Week always provided some high jinks and downright dangerous pranks but, of course, all in the name of worthy charities. Little harm was inflicted by the continuous 'snake' of students that started on the 5th.floor of our building and wended it's way downwards gathering additional personnel and, of course, money, as it journeyed through the city streets. Careering onwards with jangling collecting cans it attempted extremely awkward visits to shops, department stores and pubs intent on extracting every available penny. The beer soaked snake eventually staggered into the Students Union with it's 'cargo' but not before it had perpetrated a dastardly deed on the statue of one of the city's famous sons. It was not until the early hours of the following day that City Council officials found the end result of the high spirited students - the 'gentleman' had been dressed on skimpy red underwear! At least it was for a good cause.

Our very final studio session and 'crit' of university life, often something of a damp squib we had been told, turned out to be the highlight of the year. Having already submitted our designs for air filled plastic structures, the materials of the future, we took it in turns to describe our reasoned judgement for the design and field questions from students and tutors alike. It was always something of a nerve racking time particularly if you were a little unsure why the roof of your design appeared to be more akin to a series of inflated bananas! Tension in the crit room was suddenly replaced by heightened expectancy at the entry of one of the students, an attractive blonde and busty girl. Clad in shiny red pvc mac, black plastic boots and glossy red and black plastic mini skirt that resembled a pelmet she advanced to her crit boards and announced it was her intention to dress in harmony with her design. The young tutor's eyes shot out on stalks and his jaw dropped a mile; even the other students were speechless yet full of admiration.

What a finale!

Just plastic fantastic - far better than sausage, chips and peas!

Footnote: Jack Straw has recently been superseded as Foreign Secretary in a Tony Blair reshuffle.

WAR AND PEACE

If there is one thing I cannot abide it is being prevented from walking in places where I and many others for generations have enjoyed a long standing and historic privilege. These privileges, enshrined in British law, have been admired and adopted by countries around the world over the centuries. But we live in a rapidly changing world where privileges and rights once considered sacred are under threat - in some cases even from our own elected Members of Parliament sitting in authority in the capital.

My time in London in the mid 70's was a period of mixed blessings. Having already met my future wife, based in London for her nurse training, I made a conscious decision to work in the 'big smoke' and reduce the wear and tear on both myself and my ancient Triumph Herald. Living first in the leafy suburbs of Enfield and Palmers Green I found it convenient, although not as environmentally friendly as I had wished, to go to work each day as a patron of British Railways. The mode of travel down the 'drain' to Moorgate and the City could be likened to being transported in cattle trucks! Thankfully the monotony of daily commuting along with the ingestion of foul pollutants and the total destruction of pristine white shirts was terminated with marriage to my fiancee in our home city of Peterborough followed by honeymoon in Jersey. Neither of us looked forward to returning to London as the offer of a secure job for my wife at her hospital in the West End meant commuting all over again - something we just could not contemplate. But luck for once shone on us and we were offered a mews flat a stones throw from Oxford Circus; the down side was that it was above offices of the architectural practice for whom I worked! Fortunately I was based at their main offices in Gray's Inn which entailed a journey across central London every day. The mews flat proved to be the only stroke of luck in what turned out to be an horrific experience which eventually persuaded us to escape to the relative peace and quiet of the countryside. The flats' location had tremendous benefits not least that we could both, if we wished, walk to our work through the rag trade quarter rather than rely on the cramped and smelly tube or bus. We could also enjoy regular 'free' concerts at the Wigmore Halls at our leisure - our flat being immediately opposite its rear entrance!

The freedom to walk the capital's unsung streets and alleyways in all weathers and at all times of the year, and coming to understand and delight in it's sights, buildings and personalities, was something I particularly enjoyed. After a long, tiring day at the office in Grays Inn Square the homeward trek took me through some of the most fascinating back streets steeped in centuries of history. I felt refreshed and invigorated on my arrival at the flat - far better than being squeezed and jostled in heaving masses of humanity on the tube any day! It was at this time that I managed to purchase a copy of a book entitled 'Haunted London' by Peter Underwood which gave me an incredible insight into the weird and strange doings in the capital. One route to the flat took me past the main entrance to the Middlesex Hospital at which my wife worked and where many of the staff have been privileged, if that is the right description, to see the Grey Lady walking the wards. It seems the top half of her appears at floor level of one ward whilst her lower half is at ceiling level of the ward immediately below! Enough to question your own sanity? Apparently this seemingly strange occurrence has quite a logical explanation - the apparition is just keeping to the floor levels of a hospital building long since demolished. Tell that to the staff and patients after they have seen the Grey Lady!

After a while we took our freedom to walk the capital for granted and to such an extent that we packed off our beloved Triumph Herald to the Somerset countryside where my parents lived. The old car enjoyed a much earned rest only being used when we returned to the glorious countryside for occasional weekends. My wife had an ulterior motive for parting with the car - she was no longer prepared to suffer near mental torture and breakdown in the melee around Marble Arch!

Extended lunch hours would find me briskly heading north from Grays Inn through side streets to the Euston Road and my favourite antiquarian bookshop to spend ever increasing hours browsing through dusty old leather bound volumes. It became an enjoyable pastime until one fateful day when our rightful freedom to walk the streets unhindered was rudely shattered.

Suddenly there were people in our midst determined to destroy and take away our hard won and treasured rights. Car bombs and letter box bombs, in fact explosives planted anywhere to cause destruction, mayhem and death, became the new order. Nowhere was safe. The forays to my friendly bookseller and even to King's Cross to purchase tickets for us to travel to the in - laws in Peterborough became a dice with death. No one knew when these maniacs would strike. The final straw came one day when it felt as though the whole West End had been detonated. Our mews flat 'lifted off the ground' and miraculously returned to terra firma in one piece whilst fire and burglar alarms rang wildly and discordantly throughout the streets. It could have been several jumbo jets crash landing in Oxford Circus for the noise that was created. For the first time I now know how they must have felt in the blitz and without any thought I crazily ran from the flat to my wife's hospital not even caring for the dangers that may have lurked in parked cars or in post boxes on my route. Until that moment it would have been considered suicidal to pass within even a hundred yards of a parked car or a post box!

The public outcry was vociferous and lengthy - not unexpectedly. National and civic leaders rallied round proclaiming loud and clear their support of the people's right to freedom from the impending tyranny. It was as though, for a short while, that the country had been put on a war footing in defence of its civil liberties. But how the mighty and the powerful at the head of the nation change once the initial threat has apparently passed, whether it be from across the Irish Sea or form within our own backyard. The population is in general far more informed, educated and certainly more determined to stand up and be counted than our leaders give them credit. Many are not averse to proclaiming that our elected bodies at national and local level have got it wrong, yet again! There seems to be an all too prevalent attitude amongst our politicians of total disregard for people and places even after they have sworn and declared at the hustings their avowed intent of placing the lives and the environment of the people at the very centre of their deliberations. Is it little wonder that apparently quiet, unassuming and law abiding citizens rise up in anger and disbelief at what is about to be imposed on them with complete impunity and arrogance? History was almost repeated over the Poll Tax much to the surprise of the politicians whilst events at Newbury and Honiton by passes and the Manchester Airport extension have revealed the true feelings of the public even in the light of the 'carrots' offered - reduced travelling times of 5 minutes and some additional employment at the expense of local people's health and privacy. 'Swampy' may have appeared to take the argument to the extreme for many people but he only put into action what many people felt but did not have the courage to display - he did have a point!

Maybe only this sort of action will make our leaders sit up and take notice. It has come to a pretty impasse if we now have to 'declare war' on the very bureaucratic machinery and institutions which were created to protect our rights and freedoms from those intent on removing it!

Who would have believed it?

Peace be with you.

SLOW AND DIRTY

Our journey out of central London during the early hours of the morning burdened down, it seemed, with the worries of the whole world as well as our meagre possessions was, on reflection, the worst day of my life. It may not have seemed out of place to the residents of the metropolis or the communities along the A4 but it made us feel like refugees fleeing from the ensuing and all engulfing conflict. Ragged around the edges and feeling very sorry for ourselves we wearily dragged our tired bodies into Bath, our new home for the foreseeable future - at least until the employment market lifted and my profession was in demand once more. Unemployment is a soul destroyer and let no one else tell you differently - if you've been there you don't want to visit it again!

Bath is a fine city with architectural masterpieces peered over and dissected by vast hoards of tourists but I certainly found little enthusiasm to enjoy the flavours and delights. Wedged tightly into the Avon valley with terraced house of soft ice cream coloured stone climbing relentlessly up the steep valley sides it is steeped in history and antiquity. The Roman Baths, the Abbey, the Royal Crescent and the Pulteney Bridge are the focal point of the tourists who either reach Bath by car, bus or train.

My arrival in Bath reminded me of my first visit to the city as a child, albeit a brief one when I did not even set foot on it's streets but gasped at it's beauty and setting as I glided in by train from London Paddington. The sweep of the GWR into Bath Spa Station is etched in my memory - the proud Abbey rising above the city and the Avon lugubriously continuing its journey under the stupendous Pulteney Bridge. But as a lad I was train mad and the names of the stations - Reading General, Swindon, Chippenham, Bath Spa and Bristol Temple Meads - were sweet sounds to my ears.

I doubt few if any of the tourists who visit the city appreciate its unique importance as a railway centre, that is until Mr Beeching inflicted a disastrous blow. Bath Spa station hosted the immaculate, up market chocolate and cream coaches and gleaming brass engines of the GWR - God's Wonderful Railway - whilst Bath Green Park station was the terminus of the SDR - the Somerset and Dorset Railway. The two railway companies were poles apart yet the SDR held wonderful fascination as a rural line - it almost seemed that Mr Beeching earmarked this line for closure purely to spoil the enjoyment of those who wondered at it's charm, quaintness and indeed glorious isolation. How dare we allow ourselves to enjoy such pleasures in the 60's and 70's when there was a new push for streamlining and economising the railway companies at all costs? The engines of the SDR were a totally different breed - mixed, untidy, often unkempt in appearance and frequently borrowed from other lines. Their drivers were in a different class and not 'top line' as the GWR; they were tough, resilient, determined and fiercely patriotic to the 'Slow and Dirty' as it was colloquially called. Slow? - possibly. Dirty? - not always but definitely rural and charming and always offering surprises at the most unlikely locations. The line and its characters drew train fanatics from far and wide and in particular photographers to whom it provided spectacular scenery accompanied by even more impressive engine feats. The gradients on the line were akin to scaling Everest and were complimented by tunnels and quaintly named and decorated halts - all part of the lines' endearing qualities. By the time we had arrived in Bath from London the SDR had been gone almost 10 years but little did we realise until scanning a book in the local library that our flat stood almost directly over one of the tunnels - in fact the very first one encountered by those intrepid drivers and their steaming monsters on leaving Green Park Station. As if almost in respect for what had been we made a pilgrimage to the tunnel entrance, now peaceful and rapidly being overtaken by nature. Venturing into the city we found Green Park Station in the grips of advancing vegetation although it's fine canopy and platforms were still visible, the tracks having been lifted long ago. Templecombe, Peasedown, Gurney Slade, Temple Cloud, and Binegar Hill have all drifted into obscurity and rural peace although their names live on in books that trace the birth, life and death of what was a remarkable line.

There is even less of the Somerset and Dorset left in Bath today and I believe the site of the former Green Park Station may well be earmarked for one of those ubiquitous, bland and predictable supermarkets that so many seem to worship and adore. What is there to remind the tourist or the avid supermarket trolley pusher of the incredible engineering feat that heralded the SDR? Sadly virtually nothing. How we have lost our sense of pride and place and imaginative powers and allowed ourselves to be sucked into an anonymous and de – personalised super highway lifestyle. At least the SDR had massive helpings of personality in both human and mechanical terms. Slow and dirty it may have been dubbed in the shadow of the GWR, now itself denigrated and standardised to the point of using 'high speed bananas' as my eldest son so aptly describes them, but it could quite easily and more accurately have been described as the 'Swift and Delightful!'

ROCKIN' ALL OVER THE WORLD

As far as the eye's can see it's a mass of blue and white - scarves, hats, shirts and banners. It matters little whether you area teenager, hardened middle aged campaigner or a senior citizen - who would no doubt insist he'd seen this all before - or even a babe in arms, as everyone had to witness the 'battle'!

It seemed few if any of the 20,000 fans cared that it had been raining 'stair rods' all day, was still raining and would continue to do so even when they could drag themselves away from the celebrations and make their jubilant way home. The crowd are jubilant and good humoured with total strangers hugging and kissing and jumping skywards while the sound systems pound out the all so familiar music associated with these events. Those who were convinced they had no singing voice suddenly discover that it's not that bad after all and ecstatically join in the fun, thudding their feet in rhythm with the bass being pumped out at incredible decibels through the speakers. You can't hear yourself think let alone speak to your neighbour! The air is electric and the feeling euphoric - no one in blue and white has a care in the world. Everyone is wildly ecstatic as our team have won promotion.

'We are the champions' and 'We're going on up' reverberate around the stadium. Of course - it's Wembley! There is just nothing to compare with its atmosphere - it makes your hair stand on end!

Our football team - Peterborough United - the Posh - are at Wembley again for the second time in 8 years and we've won the Nationwide 2nd Division Play offs and made history as well. Wembley will never be used for these matches ever again as the bulldozers will shortly move in to demolish this famous piece of football history and legend to make way for a 'state of the art' stadium fit for the 21st, century. From the celebrations outsiders would think we had won the World Cup. By the time the final whistle has blown and the unbearable, nail - biting stress of the final 15 minutes and injury time has evaporated (where did that referee find those 5 minutes of additional time?) the opposition fans in their black and white have disconsolately drifted away. But we haven't noticed them leaving! As the persistent rain drifts relentlessly across the floodlights our eyes are fixed on those wonderful players, and in particular Andy Clarke the scorer of the winning goal, who proudly hold the cup aloft. What a night to remember!

Some 45 minutes later we tear ourselves away from the scenes of wild partying and head out into the miserable wet night to wend our way down Wembley Way towards the tube station. We converge with thousands of deliriously happy, well behaved fans decked out in blue and white and chanting 'Up the Boro' and 'We're going up'. Even the police horse riders exchange smiles and good humoured jokes with the fans. As we are heading north to Stanmore and the tube terminus we are still in a state of shock. We relive that crucial goal in minute detail and that nightmare 20 minutes that followed when it seemed that our team's goal led far more of a charmed life than we had wished even though our strikers could have added another 2 or 3 goals with ease. A couple sitting opposite us in the tube train, obviously supporters of our heroes on account of their scarves, were deep in conversation on the finer technical points of the match.

'Once we scored the other team were blown - their legs had gone' and ' Mind you, Faz and Ritchie could both have scored in the last few minutes - I'll never know how that 'piledriver' from Faz missed!'

That it takes us more than an hour to extract ourselves from Stanmore tube car park doesn't really matter - our journey home northwards is happy and we eventually sink into comfortable beds to await the excitement of the following day. But as we fall asleep it already is the following day!

We fall out of bed the very same morning and pinch ourselves just in case the previous night's rapture had been all a dream. The complete population of the city seems to have poured onto the streets to greet their heroes in the open topped bus - everyone wants to be a part of the celebrations! The city just grinds to a halt whilst the bus makes it's way round to the accompaniment of car horns and people dancing in the street with blue and white scarves and banners.

Days after the event the wearing of a blue and white scarf attracts the blast of horns as cars, vans and buses pass by. The feel good factor is well and truly abroad. The city is 'ROCKIN' ALL OVER THE WORLD.
UP THE POSH!!!!!!!!

AT PEACE WITH THE WORLD

Wordsworth complained almost 200 years ago that this almost self contained stubbornly independent northern outpost of England - one of the most unspoilt, precious landscapes in the British Isles - was under threat of being overrun and ruined by tourists. It has been the haven of many a poet and artist seeking solitude and inspiration in past centuries and no doubt continues to be so today. Coleridge, Southey and De Quincy with Wordsworth, the Lakes poets, and visiting figures such as Walter Scott, Keats, Lamb, Shelley and Ruskin and of course latterly Beatrix Potter (or Mrs Hedis as she preferred to be known) have al eulogised on the Lakes mystical, often hidden and unappreciated qualities. For how long will the English Lakes survive unscathed from the ever spreading and unsympathetic ravages of our modern world? Kendal, Keswick, Windermere, Ambleside, Ravenglass, Coniston, Hawkshead and the odd name of a Lakeland peak are known to most and, dare I say probably far too many. Thankfully few have sought some of the more isolated, unsung, off the beaten track hamlets and churches - and long may it remain this way!

The family - that is our two golf mad sons - had decided they needed to put a Lakeland course to the test and headed for the links at Grange over Sands. The youngest pleaded with his mother to caddy and with the oldest quite capable of steering his own bag and trolley around the windswept 18 holes this conveniently left me to head north and explore the truly wild and uncompromising countryside and it's buildings - well away from the queues of foul smelling vehicles clogging town and village and incessant hoards of tourists!

Cartmel Fell Church is the most evocative and secluded setting anyone could wish for. Its only companions are the village hall lying just outside the lychgate, a few ancient and ragged sheltering oaks and of course the broad expanse of bracken covered fells. The journey to the church is nonetheless fascinating as cars and coaches are thankfully few and far between on the narrow winding country lanes - it is quite likely few of the 'visitors' would recognise the timelessness and history of the landscape they were passing. I pass High and Low Tarn Farms that display a functional dignity in the rugged farmhouse and barns clustered protectively around a courtyard seeking warmth and security to the south across the Winster Valley - Thorplinsty Hall, Swallow Mire, Hodge Hill, Bowland Bridge, Strawberry Bank and the ancient farmsteads of Burblethwaite and Cowmire Halls - names that have survived centuries of change whilst much else is lost forever without any record. The Pele Tower attached to Cowmire Hall is a reminder of what was a troubled past some six centuries ago when Scottish raiding parties were all too common and residents retreated behind the 5 feet thick stone walls until the marauders lost interest and gave up their quest.

Something you do not expect in such a remote area is to happen upon some 20 or so persons quietly and contentedly sitting in a country churchyard eating their 'docky' and chewing the cud. That I was surprised is an understatement but I know they were just as taken aback by my appearance in this remote corner of the county. As members of a local Ramblers Group they were on a well trodden route and frequently only met the occasional farmer and some hill sheep but regularly called at the Church to take their rest on ancient stone slab seats set on the warm south facing side of the building. The church interior is cool, calm and rustic with charming ancient crucifix, pulpit and pews - two of the pews, I discover, are the manorial seats of none other than the families of Cowmire and Burblethwaite dating back some 400 years! Soaking up the tranquillity I decide I must take my leave of the ramblers and sneak another longing look at the breathtaking landscape that surrounds this most glorious corner of the kingdom.

I know I must return to Grange and collect the golfers before we all head off for the bleak and wild landscape of Hardknott and Wrynose. But I feel I must have another look at this unpretentious seaside town which owed it's prosperity to the Furness Railway that hugs the coastline on it's picturesque way from Whitehaven and Barrow to Carnforth and Lancaster. This quiet little resort with it's fine clock tower still holds some of the old fashioned gentile charm in it's houses and hotels bedecked in summer with colourful hanging baskets - something that has sadly been lost from many of our seaside towns.

Bags and trolleys loaded we make tracks past Ulverston and Broughton across the Duddon Valley, alongside the brooding Devoke Water and descend into Eskdale to Boot at the head of the Ravenglass and Eskdale Railway. Although tack and the worst side of tourism have even blighted some of the most attractive and unique places within the Lake District thankfully the dedicated band of workers on this former narrow gauge mineral line that meanders gently down to Ravenglass have managed to strike the right balance - something of a rarity I must admit. It's certainly worth taking time out for a return journey 'back in time' on this little gem if only to admire the ever changing landscape of the 'lake less' Eskdale from it's grandeur of the fells and Stanley Ghyll Force to the peaceful meadows and woodlands of the estuary as it meets the coast at the Roman Fort 'Glannaventa' - 'the market by the shore' - modern day Ravenglass.

My return to Dalegarth Station, near Boot, was in some trepidation as I knew that I would be cajoled into making the hair - raising climb and descent of the 'savage' Hardknott and Wrynose Passes in order to reach Ambleside. It brought back vivid memories of my father in laws tortuous attempts many years ago when he urged his ancient Austin Cambridge to reach these same dizzy heights and descend the perilous hairpins all in the name of a holiday 'jaunt'. The climb up the corkscrewing pass of Hardknott, avoiding the Herdwick sheep which seem intent on 'parking' themselves at the most inconvenient point on the unfenced mountain road, is quite an experience for the passengers but possibly the worst sort of experience for the ill fated driver! Having felt that all your 'lives' as a driver had been used up in the ascent you reach the summit and some of the wildest and remote countryside in the land. My eldest son, having consulted the Ordnance Survey map, proudly announced that we had been travelling along the course of a Roman military road and that I would have to follow the Romans again down the other side to reach Little Langdale! I thought the Romans were renowned for their straight roads not tortuous hairpins! Away to our left and just below the craggy outcrops of Border End lies what must surely have been the most lonely and inhospitable outpost in the whole Roman Empire - Hardknott Fort - Mediobogdum or 'the fort in the middle of the bend'. The views are dramatic and stunning whichever way you look - to the west, looking down Eskdale, the wilderness is dominated by Scafell Ridge, Bowfell and Crinkle Crags whilst to the east across Wrynose lie the Langdale Pikes with the outline of Helvelyn, Scardale and Rydale Fells showing their splendour and magnificence amongst the mist and low cloud. The place is bleak, wild and uncompromising and yet a deep and inner peace reigns. I am dragged back to the quest and assault in hand - I'm not going to be given an opportunity to escape! If you needed nerve, a good handbrake and a head for heights on the ascent of Hardknott then a steel will, utter faith in your footbrakes and the holding power of your engine plus a large amount of blind stupidity are the order of the day for the descent of Wrynose - the hairpins and gradients are something far beyond most people's wildest nightmares! I just hope those Romans had a good set of brakes on their carts and horses!

It is a relief, particularly to the driver, to realise the worst of the ordeal is over as we reach Fell Foot Farm, a wonderful Lake District vernacular farmhouse with it's two storied front porch. Once an inn, it served as a resting point for packmen and their animals before the arduous accent over Wrynose and down the Hardknott into the Esk or Duddon Valleys. It's not hard to see the little building's importance for animals and packmen travelling in either direction - it could quite easily be a modern day watering hole for motorists seeking rest and calm having achieved the dizzy heights and 'Dutch courage' for those about to embark upon the challenge. For those of a nervous disposition this venture across the Hardknott and Wrynose is something to be avoided!

Feeling drained of energy and trying to come to terms with relatively flat roads we decide against Ambleside and detour across country with the help of our eldest son's map reading skills through Skelwith Bridge, past the Drunken Duck and Outgate to Hawkshead at the head of Esthwaite Water. Pleasing to the eye and picturesquely set in the vale overlooked by Grizedale Forest the village, formed of informal clusters of ancient whitewashed and slate roofed houses grouped around courtyards, alleyways and squares, has gained immeasurably from recent pedestrianisation. But just like Coniston, Ambleside, Grasmere and Windermere it suffers from a surfeit of tourists and the trappings that unfortunately go with them - the links with the likes of Wordsworth and Beatrix Potter I'm certain add to some of the more unseemly and unsavoury 'tourist clobber' that appears at every corner and in many shop windows. Wordsworth would turn in his grave if he knew what they were perpetrating in his name!

One thing is certain there is no lack at Hawkshead or elsewhere in the Lake District, of being reminded that walking and hiking across fells and hills is big business despite the well-documented and understandable concerns of the National Park. Damage caused by both holidaymakers and weekend visitors to recognised footpaths, bridleways and lanes must be regarded as a national if not a worldwide problem - but that is another story.

In spite of all this there are still many 'hidden' places left that are glorious in their isolation and wildness where you can be at peace with the world.

CALL IT A TUSCAN COUNTRY

The calling bell rings out across the sleepy countryside from the collegiate church of Casole D'Elsa as it has done for generations. Set high on a hill at the centre of a quaint and fascinating fortified village surrounded by olive groves and vineyards it is out of our sight. A sea of saffron yellow sunflowers nod gently and turn their heads to the searing midday sun; row upon row of vines and olives 'walk' inexorably in serried ranks up the sun drenched sides of the valley. Clusters of ancient terracotta roofed farmsteads with brilliant whitewashed walls gleam brightly across the hillside.

Everything sleeps in the heat of a sun pouring it's powerful rays down out of a cloudless azure blue sky. The only movement comes from a flock of sheep; the sound of the leader's clanging bell seems to rise and fall as the woolly mass head erratically, pausing for the occasional nibble of a tasty morsel, down the slopes to find better pasture and shelter from the punishing heat. It's siesta time - and it seems to last all day!

The food and wine is excellent as is the Tuscan weather - so long as you choose early morning or late afternoon to make your holiday forays into city, town or hillside village. Any other time will send you rapidly in search of shade and an ice cool drink although some tourists appear to ignore the locals' habit of 'shutting up shop' for an extended break of often 3 hours or more. Red, sore and peeling bodies continue to walk the streets or lie like boiled lobsters beside swimming pools seemingly oblivious to the time honoured siesta of relaxing in the shade.

The intrinsic beauty of Tuscany truly lies in it's evocative farmsteads and hillside hamlets and towns grouped, as always, around a small church with the weather beaten calling bell sheltering under it's own bright orange pantile roofed cote. They fit so naturally into the timeless countryside as if they could only have been organically grown - they are in total harmony with their setting and with the local community portray a wonderful sense of 'belonging'. Could anything be closer than man, nature and faith working in complete unison? Venture into the ice cool interior of one of these rural churches and gaze upon the amazing frescoes that are everywhere - ceilings, walls and pillars - they are a delight to behold. The stunningly slow pace of life in this almost forgotten world is an enduring experience.

Most tourists head for, and recount endlessly through cine film and camera, the main centres of Sienna, Pisa and Florence now totally dominated by hoards of sightseers and line upon line of honking, irate traffic. Both Florence and Sienna have recently made a decision to pedestrianise their centres to preserve their architectural and historic treasures and retain some sort of sanity for the inhabitants. In some centres pollution has reached such alarming levels that famous statues that once adorned piazzas and religious buildings have been taken inside for safety and replaced by modern copies. With persistence and perseverance, and certainly if you are an 'early bird', you can avoid the frantic search for parking and the vast numbers of tourist coaches and park on the outskirts - from here you can take a leisurely 15 minute stroll into any of these delightful cities. If the return to your car is too much to contemplate after treading the ancient streets, sampling the culinary delights and gazing in wonder at the architectural masterpieces then fear not! Hop aboard one of the many buses that seem to circumnavigate the centres in ever decreasing circles. But beware of these purveyors of weary pedestrians - they are not for the faint hearted or for those who are unsure of which direction they should be heading! They are more akin to Greek taxis, tearing around at breakneck speed but somehow still managing to arrive at their destination (and hopefully yours!) in one piece! If you're thinking of Pisa as a place of pilgrimage - forget it! The Duomo and the Leaning Tower are but isolated structures in a sea of seething traffic and anonymous streets and buildings. It is depressingly overrated!

If you must tread the tourist trail make early calls at the hilltop fortified towns of Colle di Val D'Elsa, San Gimigiano, Monteriggioni or Volterra. The 'upper' town of Colle - Colle Alta - is an incredible hillside walled fortress stretching along a ridge with it's one long street lined with medieval palazzi and a maze of narrow alleys leading off to small glass blowing workshops and fascinating trattorias all perched high above the surrounding countryside. Soak up the stunning views over local cuisine and wine. Both San Gimigiano and Volterra are definitely for the early risers if you don't want to be disappointed. Gimigiano, the 'Delle Belle Torri', is rightly famous for it's amazing skyline of medieval towers overseeing the fortified hilltop town whilst Volterra sits astride bleak yellow grey volcanic hills curiously isolated and grim amidst the surrounding gentle pastoral countryside. As D.H Lawrence aptly remarked - 'It gets all the wind and sees all the world'. Stuffed wild boars heads, the local gastronomic delicacy, stare at you from every vantage point whilst many visitors find they cannot leave without a keepsake of alabaster - every other shop seems to sell every conceivable artefact made from this locally found marble.

Maybe it is better to retire to the tranquillity of the Tuscan countryside ....the day is drawing to a close and from the villa window I can see the intense orange setting sun making it's final journey of the day below the tip of the distant hillside. It's time for a cool drink under the awning on the veranda. Everything - farmhouse, church, barn and even the hillside of vines, olives and sunflowers suddenly turn a rich golden, almost blood red as the sun takes it's bow to signal another calm and balmy evening to come. As the heat of the day subsides the wildlife emerges and springs to life triggered, it seems, by some unseen internal clock - they're not that stupid to work and play when the sun is at it's hottest! It's not just the bird population that suddenly come to life but also the ubiquitous crickets that keep up their constant calling far into the crystal clear night sky.

Under the stars we sit outside the osteria and lazily chat over the days doings and adventures whilst sipping one of the local wines and working our way through a vast selection of Tuscan delicacies. We don't want to leave and another two bottles of wine are placed on our candle lit table - but it's gone midnight and we walk contentedly the 5 minutes back to our villa and sink into a peaceful sleep. The crickets, under a star lit, balmy night sky, are determined to stay awake - no sleep for them!

This is a Tuscan country.

HEAVEN IS 'NOWHERE'

 Viewed from the air this immensely stunning and beautiful archipelago of 128 islands is set in a world of it's own. With just five inhabited islands lying 30 miles off Lands End they appear to be in the middle of 'nowhere', nestling together and connected by seemingly endless beaches of brilliant powdery white sparkling sand amidst azure blue waters. Home to just some 2000 vigorous, resourceful and independent minded islanders the Isles of Scilly are blissfully peaceful and relaxing – pure serenity – a rarity anywhere in the world.

 Exploring by boat is the essence of any stay on the islands, crossing the crystal clear waters accompanied by a host of inquisitive seals, porpoises and seabirds. Most content themselves by taking inter island launches guided by the friendly Scillonian boatmen. Whichever of the islands you land on you will find just walkers with occasional bikers and even a horse! Cars barely exist so there is no traffic noise and thumping or pounding music – just peace!

 Bryher on the far north western edge of the Scillies is inspirational – it's an island of often totally different 'wonders'. Hell Bay truly lives up to its name and is a marvel to behold when westerly gales pound in shore. The north of the island is magnificent with stunning heath lands and downs whilst to the south a relaxing walk at Rushy Bay gives the feeling at low tide of being 'tethered' to the hills of nearby uninhabited Samson and

Puffin Island. Leaving the heart of the island with it's groups of spectacular tiny white painted cottages and their small intensely exuberant sub tropical gardens I head down towards the quay on the east side of the island to another 'wonder' of Bryher – dazzling white sand and brilliantly clear shallow waters perfect for snorkelling or a lazy swim! You could even take a romantic walk through the sand carpeted shallows that appear at low tide between Bryher and Tresco. It's just wonderful!

But so is St. Agnes – it feels a 'world apart' when you land by launch at the little quay just below the well known Turks Head – a little hostelry that everyone should visit. It's reputation for amazing food and well kept ice - cold beers and scrumpy is well deserved – and the view from the pub greensward across crystal clear waters to Gugh, Samson and St.Mary's is breathtaking! A young teenage girl walks leisurely through the glass blue shallows searching for shells – something tells me she was thoroughly enjoying herself. Why not walk across the punishingly crystalline white sand bar to Gugh before it's turned into an island by the incoming tide. Relax and unwind on one of the many small sandy coves or spoil yourself by eating luscious scones and strawberry jam with thick yellow cream – courtesy of the St. Agnes cows, many of which are Jerseys.

St. Martin's must be the most outstanding island – so friendly, peaceful and timeless with crystal clear light. As you approach the Lower Town quay on the inter island launch the sight of endless beaches and calm azure water takes your breath away. The temptation to swim or snorkel in crystal clear water over parchment coloured sands is overwhelming – and there is no one else there! Walking down the island lane you cannot take your eyes off the spectacular coastal scenery of Neck of the Pool and Lawrence's Brow before you are tempted to try a cream tea with strawberries at a wonderful little cottage café.

You are spoilt for choice. Spend some time relaxing on the rocks overlooking the Old Quay and the clear blue waters across to Tresco or just wander inland to the island's only bakery and it's wonderful fayre. Walk across the island's cricket square by the wide crescent of Higher Town Bay with it's intense white beaches and seek out the vineyard run by Graham Thomas and his wife – the most southerly and westerly vineyard in Britain. I drink a refreshingly cool glass of wine and soak up the vineyard atmosphere under a baking sun whilst looking across Higher Town Bay to the Eastern Isles. Don't fail to take plenty of wine back with you as there's no Customs and Excise!

Time flies by far too fast in this 'heaven'. I take a last, long lingering look back at St. Martin's as the launch leaves to take us back to St. Mary's.

Although the largest of the islands and perhaps the one that sees the most internal combustion engines because of the Scillonian III and the heliport, St Mary's is still an awe inspiring peaceful island. With over 30 miles of scenic coastal paths and nature trails and a sub tropical climate that encourages masses of flowering succulents and other wild flowers to overwhelm granite walls and outcrops it is hardly surprising the island attracts many wildlife and wild flower enthusiasts. The most stunning and heavenly walk must be from

Porthcressa around the Penninis Headland to descend gently down to Old Town. I start my walk across the seeringly white sand of Porthcressa Beach under a clear deep blue sky and my attention is immediately taken by two people in the azure blue water – mother and son enjoying snorkelling in the shallows.

'What's it like?' I call to them

'It's cold' the mother replies.' Without a wetsuit it would be freezing. Fancy a try? We're here for the day'.

'Thanks – I might just take up your offer later' I replied.

I retraced my steps back onto Penninis Headland footpath and headed towards Old Town Bay, another idyllic setting for snorkelling, scuba diving or just plain swimming. The views from the pathway as it meanders and hugs the cliff edge is stunning – wonderful seascapes and rock formations as well as an array of wildflowers, lichens and bird life. The descent into Old Town alongside the bay, Gull Rock and over to Tolman Point is beyond belief – the sands and azure waters certainly live up to reputation. So carried away with the view I almost miss the little church virtually hidden amidst the vegetation. This is the last resting place of former Prime Minister Sir Harold Wilson who wisely spent most of his holidays in the locality. I walk on around the bay and call in at small beachside café for an ice cool drink before reluctantly retracing my steps along the headland footpath towards Porthcressa. To my surprise and pleasure the snorkellers were still there and after a baking hot walk I was definitely in need of cooling off.

'You're back' called out the boy.

'Yes, and I wouldn't mind having a go' I replied.

With his mother taking care of all my expensive camera gear I kitted up in her wetsuit, some 2 sizes too big, mask, fins and snorkel and swam out with her son into the clear shallow waters. It was an exhilarating experience and as we finished and waded out of the sea carrying our fins he charged up the beach to his mum flapping his arms in the air with obvious excitement.

'That was really great! Can we do it again tomorrow?'

Turning to me he just said

'Thanks so much – you were super!'

On my final day on the Scillies I decided I would take up the suggestion of one of the guests in the hotel and head for the Old Town Inn – apparently a purveyor of fine food, beers and ciders. The 'short cut' footpath to Old Town passes near Buzza Tower – the highest point for some miles. I pause for a moment on the very steep path and take in the unbelievable views across to St Agnes and Gugh and to Samson and Tresco before continuing my descent to Old Town from a totally different direction.

My eyes suddenly fall upon a delightful tiny white cottage with a red telephone box in the garden!! I cannot take my eyes off the cottage and it's wonderful, natural and unmanicured layout complete with displays of 'Scilly Sea Urchins'. A white and black painted timber sign pointing towards the blue cottage door says simply – 'Nowhere'. But who would own such a glorious piece of nostalgia? Having taken a few photos through the blue painted wicket gate I decide I must seek the permission of the owners and I head round the cottage onto the track that looks across the stunning Old Town

Beach out to Gull Rock. To my surprise all I can find is a timber building with the name 'Island Seas Safaris' affixed and giving details of seas safaris, snorkelling with seals and Gig Racing trips. With no one around my mind turns to a cool refreshing drink and in a scorching noon day heat I retrace my way to the end of Old Town Beach and the Inn which had been my original quest. My luck is out as there are no staff to cook the Inn's stupendous food but I do down an ice cool pint of cider. Feeling much refreshed I turn out into the scorching heat of the day and head back to 'Nowhere'. I'm finally in luck as I notice several people 'kitting up' in wetsuits to venture out on a 'snorkelling with seals' trip under the expert guidance of Mark and Susie Groves. Time is limited but Susie is quite happy that I do extensive photographs of their stupendous cottage garden whilst they prepare to marvel at the 'garden under the sea'. Mark and Susie know full well I shall be back and share with them in their underwater and terra firma 'heavens' – nothing would stop me!!!!

. The Scillies are 'heaven' and 'heaven' is blissfully peaceful and stunningly beautiful.

HEAVEN IS 'NOWHERE'.

The donkeys with owner David Smith on the beach at Weston super Mare

Looking towards the former Knightstone Theatre and Baths, Weston super Mare

The Grand Pier, Weston super Mare

The donkeys by the Grand Pier, Weston super Mare

Woodwalton Church, far from it's village, on a hillock above the Fens

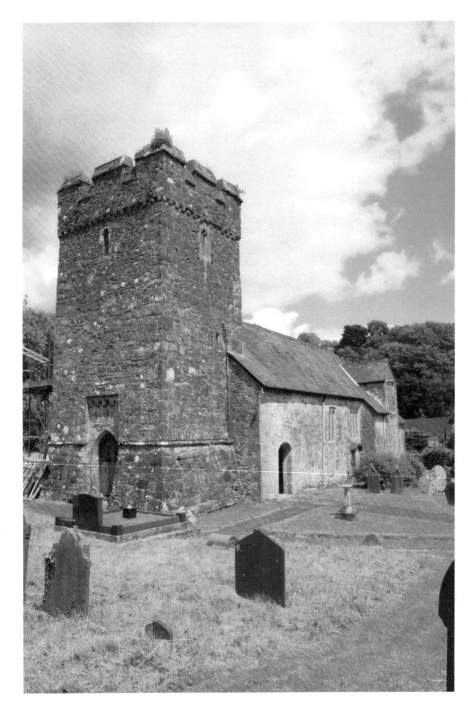

The Church of St. Egwad, Llanfynydd

Cartmel Fell Church, Lake District

A Class 4F prepares to leave Peterborough East under elevated signalbox

*The crowd cheering victorious Posh at the Division 2 Play Off Final
at Wembley May 2000*

*Eldest son Chris
celebrating at the
Wembley victory May 2000*

Recent action of the Posh (blue kit), London Road Stadium, Peterborough Utd. F.C.

The South Stand, London Road Stadium, Peterborough Utd. F.C.

'Nowhere' amidst the lillies, Old Town, St. Mary's, Isles of Scilly

The cottage garden through the wicket gate at 'Nowhere', Old Town, St. Mary's, Isle of Scilly

Old Town Church form footpath alongside Old Town Bay, St. Mary's, Isle of Scilly

The Greenwich Meridian sign alongside the Old Nene, Flood's Ferry

St. Martin's looking across to Tresco, Isles of Scilly

V

RURAL
MATTERS

OZONE AND ALL

As smoke lazily curled from chimney pots of cottages in our village one fine summer evening I pondered on our changing climate whilst 'watching the world go by' from my perch high up in the Top Meadow. Below, our sheep with their 'patchwork' lambs contentedly went about their daily routine of being 'lawnmowers', little knowing that weaning time was close when the whole valley echoed to the doleful bleatings as ewe and lamb vainly called for each other.

Returning to smoking chimneys I wondered if there would come a time when those authoritarian bureaucrats would impose urban smokeless zones on villages and rural communities in the misapprehension that the few remaining coal and wood burning houses were the perpetrators of our dramatic climate changes. That would mean our old friend in the village, who always has a log fire and regularly 'winds up' huge bonfires in his back garden would be a law breaker of the highest magnitude. Even our occasional bonfire would be outlawed along with our log fires that we look forward to so much of a winter evening.

Maybe our scientific skill and knowledge has come too late to save us from what some say will be a catastrophe of enormous proportions. Although we still drive cars too much and fail to share our vehicles, use fridges and freezers that spew out unseen chemicals and 'support' industries that have no green or environmental record whatsoever much of the damage to that small yet so significant layer in our atmosphere has been inflicted since the industrial revolution lifted off in this country. It's not that long ago, and certainly within my memory, that London and many other cities suffered the most appalling 'smogs' along with terrifying health problems. Industrial haze and smoke hung thick over houses large and small whether in the industrial heartland of Yorkshire and Lancashire or the Welsh Valleys. The memory of loosing my way home one day from Grammar School in a 'peasouper' and the terror that struck me when I ran into a very large tree still haunts me. Being caught once I walked my bicycle the rest of the way in an eerie silence and all pervading yellowy grey gloom occasionally meeting the glimmer of a light moving erratically towards me as it's owner walked with care in front of a long line of crawling vehicles. It was almost a return to the days of the flagmen when new fangled trains and automobiles were considered far too dangerous for the public without being preceded by a red flag. Thank god the days of the 'peashooters' are gone! Nonetheless we must not be complacent. The expansion of car ownership and consequent carbon emissions in the last 30 years and apparent disregard by the population and government to come to terms with the 'noose' that is tightening around us is disturbing.

Each generation rightly demands higher standards and thankfully there are signs, albeit small, that just a few are beginning to wake up and take notice. But have we come too late to a crisis that has been brewing gently like a cauldron for so long? In the few years that we have been 'involved' with the land in Wales there has been a noticeable change to what has always been recognised as an equitable climate with readily defined seasons. You can forget the seasons now for they have merged and in their place have come violent surges in the weather causing havoc to the normal and expected pattern of growth to the grass. The 12 years or so we have been in residence in Wales has been the warmest on record – and the rate of change is speeding up. It has been estimated that temperatures will rise by 5 degrees centigrade within the next 50 years – at the very moment my sons will be 'winding down' as pensioners! Trees and shrubs accustomed to our recent equitable climate will have to 'move North' at the rate of 200 miles every decade if they are to survive – that is ten times faster than in the '90's, the past decade. It is certainly a very sobering thought. But the consequences go far deeper than might first be imagined. The cost of feeding stock - cows and sheep - must rise as grass fails to grow at the right time whilst the humidity and deluges of rain cause mayhem with the feet of sheep and cost a fortune to rectify. Oh for some good old fashioned winter frosts that will kill off all those nasty bugs and beetles! Farmers and landowners are often blamed for complaining that whatever the weather they are hard done by and suffer from rapidly falling incomes. For once farmers are speaking the truth however hard it may be for politicians and urban dwellers to accept - life is very tough up in those hills of Wales, the Lake District and Scotland. The effect on your weekly shopping bill will be more than noticeable as we enter the early years of the millennium. Who needs rural decline and depopulation when the weather does it for you?

Our 'green and pleasant land' WILL change dramatically over the next generation and we no longer have any control over this. Scenes that we have all come to love and admire and take for granted will be lost - because we are too greedy and don't appear to care!

All we can do now is be better carers of our present for a tolerable future.

Hopefully I shall still be able to watch the smoke curling from those cottage chimneys for many years to come - ozone and all!

HAIRY NED

How many of us can remember those idyllic thatched cottages set amidst a gloriously wild yet wonderful garden with the ever present cat or dog standing like a sentinel at the partly open wooden hand gate? Sadly it is a fast disappearing scene in village and hamlet as the galloping global economy engulfs everything in its path.

Yet I can recall many such a scene immortalised on a box of chocolates, a packet of fudge, or tin of biscuits and even a jigsaw frequently displayed in serried ranks in old post office and village stores. We may well drool over the box of chocolates and it's idyllic village scene but more often than not we are thinking of the contents rather than the threat to the cottage and it's thatched 'hat' depicted so artistically. There's trouble at them thar' thatchers!

Twenty years ago we decided to shoulder responsibility for a tiny cottage that had been disgracefully allowed to loose it's dignity but amazingly still sported the remains of a thatched 'hat'. It was a delight to cast the eye upon - a truly special example of local traditional craftsmanship. During the course of re thatching we noticed that an old gentleman became a regular visitor at the garden gate, looking intently with admiration and curiosity at the men on the roof. Each cold winter morning, complete with woolly gloves and a scarf pulled tight around his neck, he would stand and gaze at the thatchers almost as if he were reliving the work. It transpired that he had worked on our cottage some 50 or 60 years previously. Whilst wiping away a tear from his eye with working mans hands now racked with arthritis he remarked

'I laid this thatch and that's my mark there on the eaves'.

He pointed to the straw eaves roll which I now know to be his 'signature' - the sign of a true craftsman.

'It's all gone now' he muttered 'but it's nice to see you putting a new hat on the old place'.

Fred Oldfield was an old fashioned craftsman who lived his job and put something of his very being into the craft he so passionately cared for. Sadly Fred is no more and his small thatching firm in the town of Whittlesey is also gone along with their unique thatching dialect. What replaced Fred's famous eaves rolls? Just a lump of treated softwood called an arris rail - how boring and unimaginative!

In Wales few examples of traditional thatching remain but the death knell had already been struck as far back as the start of the 20th.century when farmers and landowners bowed to economic pressure replacing thatched and draughty out of fashion properties with a new image - slated roofs at half the cost. Perhaps our modern day disease of standardisation and cheapness at the expense of long held and trusted traditions is nothing new! Some may say, quite rightly, what's amiss with a good slate roof?

Everyone instantly recognises thatch but few have any meaningful understanding of this, the most ancient of traditional crafts, that can be traced back to long before the birth of Christ. It remains a mysterious craft wrapped in strange names and terms which seem to have little meaning or relevance in our high tech world - liggers, sways, spars and slats are all in a days work for a thatcher.

Yet we stand at the gateway to the millennium and traditional thatching is facing extinction and none more so than in Wales. Apart from the fine examples in the Museum of Welsh Life it has become an endangered species only rarely coming to light under a layer of rusting corrugated iron. The unhealthy invasion of a fully developed straw thatch, more akin to Southern England, is only too apparent when you fall upon the smooth, pristine, sharp edged thatch complete with 'straw peacocks' affixed to the ridge, sitting astride a rough stone cottage. This unwelcome encroachment is certainly not part of the rural Welsh thatching tradition! In parts of West Wales the 'shaggy dog' thatch was often extended to incorporate and form the chimney and then all was held together by a network of ropes criss - crossing the roof and secured by large stones at the eaves. It's not difficult to see why this 'organic' roof was frequently likened to 'knitting' on a gigantic scale! This 'logical' approach did at least offer some assurance to the owner that he would at wake up in the morning to find he still had a roof! In these western approaches where winds are regularly at gale force or worse it was not uncommon to discover your roof had 'flown away' during the night. One old thatcher told me that he compared working on the old Welsh thatch roofs to darning a very large sock! Sadly I am told by an authoritative source in Ireland that the rope once commonly used across the Celtic countries has now been replaced by an imported sisal cord known as 'hairy ned'. Is nothing sacred?

You can however be assured that once in place your 'organic' thatch roof might well last up to 30 years or more depending on the quantity of rain and strength of the wind. With thick walls, small windows and a sound 'hat' warmth is guaranteed without the need for UPVC windows and the inevitable double - glazing. Thatch is the most successful and yet ancient form of insulation keeping it's inhabitants cosy in winter and cool in the hottest of summers - and I can vouch for this. What more could you wish for?

Autumn is without doubt the best season for corrugated iron or 'tin' hunting. Locating a distant 'tin' roof is one thing - planning your safest route to an almost certain thatched building is not so easy. Many lanes and tracks can cause havoc to the undercarriage of your most precious car and are certainly not for the faint hearted. More often than not though the perilous journey is well worth the risks.

Praise be the man who discovered and made 'tin' - without it not even 'hairy ned' would have been invented!

DOWN THE GARDEN PATH

From time immemorial all nations and their people have struggled endlessly with their consciences over the thorny issue of toilets and the products that emanate therefrom.

Neolithic man had a simple solution to this most vexing of problems - when the build up of rubbish and bodily wastes became offensive he picked up his chattels and set up home further away. Quite wrongfully many assume that the Victorians were the instigators of the privy or the ty bach as well as the foul water drain which assisted with the removal of unwanted matter. The Romans, god bless them, can, as usual, take the credit for the simple privy and it's long, illustrious and often right royal history through the intervening centuries. The principles of privies, latrines and drains may well have been 'removed' from the Greeks presumably during Roman forays into their lands. But the Roman legacy was ignored and unappreciated for centuries, our countrymen preferring to live in squalor until the privy and it's fortified companion the garderobe were conveniently re invented and used with great pomp and state by the highest in the land. Perhaps we should concede that the Victorians did at least introduce public sewerage on a large scale to compliment the privy in the largest of towns and cities although the countryside remained firmly stuck with almost prehistoric sanitation.

The Oxford Dictionary quaintly describes the privy as 'the place for easing nature' - far nearer the truth when we consider the location of many of these unsung little buildings which developed their own brand of architecture. Whether in the middle of a field, astride a stream, on the edge of a cliff or even in a church tower they displayed a quaint rural vernacular feel and personal touch. In many instances the personality of the user was evident from the names they used to describe a visit down the garden path. Imagine a privy being called the House of Commons, Windsor Castle or the Long Drop! Some cottagers, particularly in medieval times, did not possess such a grand sounding edifice - they relieved themselves in a field just a bow shot from their hovel.

Privies came in all sorts of combinations, types and sizes - some were just downright Heath - Robinsonish in their quirky features and fixtures. Some were single seaters, others double, triple and even up to 6 seats where they were quite frequently graded according to size of seat, opening and height above ground. This 'personalization' could accommodate everyone in your family or all your neighbours in the street from the smallest to the largest! It has been recorded that one three seater privy was shared by some 40 people - a true case of bringing the community closer together!

Over many years the humble yet honourable privy developed unique and individualistic methods of waste collection - from common vaults to basic holes and later the tarred timber bucket or galvanised pail. To reduce the presence of smells ingenious chute devices were sometimes fitted which, when a lever was pulled, would release ash or earth onto the container or hole in the ground. As was human nature the need to regularly empty the bucket or clean out the pit was put off as long as possible - who could blame them? If clearance only took place once a year some 90 bucket loads were often removed. Carting such a quantity away had to be very carefully planned particularly if the work was undertaken on a Sunday. Trying to avoid the congregation or the Vicar leaving after Holy Communion at the Parish Church was a fine art. Even if the fully indentured 'buckateer' did succeed in avoiding the crowd there could be little doubt, even from what was considered a safe distance, what business he was about.

Many can still remember the ghostly visit of the night soil cart, or fromarty as my father called it, outlined in the eerie glow of the old hurricane lamps as brave local men went about their duty emptying buckets from privies before heading for some specially selected field to deposit the night's takings!

Contrary to popular belief royalty also needed to 'ease nature' and engaged inventors and experts of their day to provide the most regal accommodation possible. Queen Elizabeth I had Sir John Harrington design her a flushing water closet described by the inventor as a ' privy of perfection'. It is quite likely that it was no more than an up market privy provided with a bucket of water to flush the contents through a chute into the street or the moat - as far away as possible from the Queen! Although Elizabeth I apparently had good relations with her privy two of our kings certainly did not. George II, it is recorded, let out a sound louder than the normal 'royal wind' and departed this life - literally on the throne! James II of Scotland fared even worse. Hiding from his pursuers in a privy he thought he heard the voices of friends come to save him. On lifting his head from the hole he pleaded 'Please help me from this stinking mess' - and was promptly run through with a sword by one of his enemies.

Sanitation has advanced rapidly over the past 70 - 80 years although even today some isolated properties still rely on a privy quite frequently at the bottom of the garden. Many privies still survive whether through pure luck or a deliberate attempt by the owner to keep them, possibly for sentimental reasons, but albeit in a rundown and neglected condition - a reminder of past happy days when, if you had to go, you had to go down the garden path. Nowadays there is no need to spend time cutting old newspapers into squares to hang on a nail on the back of the privy door that inevitably leaked gallons of rainwater and offered little protection from howling gales. Long gone is the need for an urgent walk down the path in pitch blackness with flickering candle or faltering old cycle lamp to reach the 'thunder box' only to find it already occupied - by the local hedgehog or cat.

Many privies have succumbed and returned from whence they came whilst a few, and probably far more than we realise, have survived as empty shells denoting a past active life. Some have even been reincarnated as potting sheds or garden stores. They are gone but not forgotten. Today's gardeners really don't know what they are missing - 'bloomin' 'jynormus' vegetables!'

Hail to thee blithe privy.

WHAT ROT !

We live in troubled times.

If your carefully tended compost heap is less than 270 yards from your back door then you could be in deep trouble. At the least you could be asked to move it, have it 'assessed' or even be forced to apply for a licence! Remember to have a lawyer well versed in the do's and don'ts of compost heaps standing by as you could quite easily be convicted under the Animal By Products Amendment Order and have to pay a fine of up to £5000!

Many would consider this to be one huge joke. How could anyone seriously believe that bureaucrats would have the audacity and nerve to invade the privacy of your garden and question where and what we put in our compost heaps. The benign ritual of throwing out potato peelings, the remains of a lettuce or cabbage and decaying flower heads onto a gently steaming and rotting pile at the bottom of the garden is an age old process that has remained unchanged for centuries.

The same hypocrisy and humbug is also about to be inflicted upon us over the impending threat to the precious Green Belt that encircles and cloaks our main centres of population. There is little doubt we have a major crisis over where we are to live in the next half century in our already crowded island and what to do with the seemingly insatiable demand for roads and vast extensions to runways and terminals of the major airports. I maybe mistaken or have read the wrong script but our government appears to be running scared that this country will be left behind by other European nations who have committed themselves to the rape of their countryside in a big way and will thus gain immeasurably in economic terms. It's panic stations in Whitehall! Yes, we need more affordable housing for those who keep our essential services in the big cities ticking over but at what price now and to our children? Ministers would do well to stand back and think long and hard before they sweep away rights enshrined in the Town and Country Planning Act 1947 and it's successors - those that give you and I the legitimate right to oppose development, on planning and environmental grounds, and take part in Public Enquiries. The current 'presidential' style government is dangerously close to implementing policies that will, at a swipe, remove these long held rights alongside their latest 'wheeze' - a far more dangerous and sinister ploy - the removal of trial by jury in many court cases which will cut at the very heart of Habeas Corpus ! And all to save a few pennies.

But back to the 'rights' of my compost heap!

Of course now that the dastardly deed has been seized upon by the media the Environment Agency are becoming increasingly embarrassed, insisting that they do not want to stamp out our lovingly cared for worm heaps but rather those in large public gardens. If you and I are not being regularly 'felled' by escaping bacteria then why should it be any different for those close to Hyde Park, Kew Gardens or even the grounds of the most avid organic evangelist HRH Prince of Wales at Highgrove in deepest Gloucestershire? A certain

Thomas Hill writing in the 16th century recommended the dung of doves and goats to condition soil and some 100 years later John Evelyns, the diarist, swore on pigeon and sheep droppings as the best material for fertilising fruit. The combinations were endless - ash, straw, leaves, grass and even weeds!

The preposterous proposals fly in the face of recognised and well documented Government and European Union policy requiring a huge shift to composting and recycling vast amounts of kitchen and garden rubbish that more often than not end up in overflowing and increasingly rare landfill sites - with, it should be said, immediate and long term threats to our health. According to the Government Order compost must not be spread on land where wild animals and birds may gain access to the heaving bacteria and spread it ad nauseam - that certainly is the end of us casting our wonderful sheep manure from the pens onto our garden around roses and fruit trees! What really angers the keen gardener and composter about attempts to curb the public spirited recycling instincts is that we are not irresponsible with our precious compost heaps - cooked vegetables, meat and cheese are taboo unless you want to encourage vermin! Why must politicians interfere with everything?

My massive compost heap is just 35 yards from the farmhouse back door and I'm not giving it up - and that's final!

What rot!

Footnote: I believe the legislation relating to compost heaps may well have been 'adjusted' as politicians so aptly word it due to the massive public outcry – if any reader knows the current situation perhaps they would contact me.

MORGUES AND MOWERS

It was always a pleasure to call at our solicitor's office in one of the quietest streets in the cathedral city where I spent most of my childhood. The street was not unlike the Minster Precincts - a peaceful haven hidden from view from the old Market Place beyond the Becket Chapel gateway. Almost every building in Priestgate, or Lawyers Row as many would've called it, was adorned with a suitably engraved brass plaque announcing who resided within its hallowed walls.

Immediately opposite the front door stood the imposing and venerable facade of the Peterborough City Museum shaded by a row of fine lime trees. Once the city infirmary I recall cycling past this fine edifice each day from school and wondering long and hard about the words printed in black on the face of one of the minor buildings to the rear – 'Decontamination'. I was probably far too young to appreciate its significance. Still to this day in one area of the museum, sadly not open to the general public, there is a very light and airy white glazed tiled room - the operating theatre - complete with 'table' and the sawdust box beneath to catch the dripping contents during operations!

Medical museums are apparently the latest tourist attraction to capture the imagination of the public with one complex recently being opened in Leeds; obviously we have a morbid curiosity in exactly what does go on in the mysterious world of medicine. Organisers of these museums advise me that it is their intention to help the man in the street to be more aware of and develop a greater insight into the National Health Service - apart from displaying the downright macabre and inhumane treatments and instruments of the past! Thank god for anaesthetics! With cavernous Victorian hospitals and institutions becoming surplus to the health service in ever increasing numbers I can see that Medical Museums will be the very place to visit with grandma one sunny afternoon. Maybe we could sit in the operating theatre and enjoy an iced bun and a cup of tea!

A similar venture into the health of our nation was recently planned at Carmarthen, our county town. To the disgust of many locals who had either been born in the building or experienced hernia or tonsils removal under the great skill of the local surgeon, it became clear that their beloved Infirmary could well be demolished. For better or for worse I was invited as a specialist in the treatment of ailing buildings to 'put my eye' over the offending structure. The enthusiasm of another expert on seeing the morgue was astonishing as he became 'lost' in all the antiquated and fascinating equipment naturally designed to assist the most ardent up and coming pathologist in their often gruesome work of post mortems. It turned out that he was none other than a famous Home Office pathologist whose life had been devoted to peering and cogitating over horrific, mutilated and decaying bodies.

'Strange' he said quietly, deftly picking up a lethal looking instrument. 'Strange what people will do to others in the name of love - I must have seen it all'.

My solicitor, reclining gracefully in his red leather chair, had also seen it all - and not just legal entanglements!

'What people will do in the name of mowers'!

'Don't talk to me about mowers' moaned John.

An excellent lawyer and adviser and a great person to listen to, he was an avid tennis fan and prided himself on the quality and velvet texture of the grass at his village residence west of Peterborough. But as he came to discover only too well there is a penalty to pay for keeping such greenswards in tip top order. Before I was able to leave his office one morning it became crystal clear that John had something of major significance to tell me - and I was persuaded to listen for a few moments to his tale of two mowers.

Determined as he was to have the best and most convenient appliance for the work in hand he had acquired a tractor mower upon which he could ride around the lawns in comfort and style. Not to put a finer point on it - it was a super GT model! He always stored his pride and joy in the large garden shed which, of course, had the biggest and best padlock attached to it. Fancying one day that he would leave the office slightly earlier than usual with the purpose of mowing his lawn on arriving home he opened the shed to find - no mower! As John so eloquently put it 'I was miffed if not a trifle annoyed'.

Accepting this as a one off experience and with cash in hand from the insurers John duly visited his local garden centre and purchased an identical machine. Resolute that he should not be outsmarted again by the mobile mower thieves he asked a friend, who so happened to own a company producing steel chains and hawsers, to supply him with the necessary 'gear' to secure his new mower. The new mower 'lived' in the shed once more but this time had several new companions - not least, one steel and one concrete grass roller and lengths of high tensile chain and hawser! The whole was wrapped and threaded through and about the shed, the mower and the rollers and complimented by the toughest anti bolt cropping padlock. John now felt quite at peace to go to work and return home for mowing his lawns with total confidence. How wrong he was! This time everything vanished - mower, rollers, chains, hawsers and padlock - save only the remnants of the garden shed left in glorious isolation in the middle of the uncut lawn!

The police told him he lived in the wrong place - within half a mile of the A1 road where, apparently, groups of thieves were passing pleasant hours removing mowers (rollers and ......chains.......)from garden sheds from under the very noses of the owners. I rapidly pictured a scene of convoys of trucks ploughing their way north and south along the A1 loaded to the rafters with mowers and ....garden gnomes with fishing rods! John made a rapid decision - not to buy another mower but hire his next door neighbour's machine and throw the garden gnomes that remained into the dustbin! John has recently made an even wiser decision - move to Portugal away from those mad mower thieves.

The moral of this salutary tale - if you must go out to mow use 4 legged mowers!

ENDANGERED SPECIES

One thing is certain whichever age or generation you live in there is always some good cause that wishes to save an endangered species.

More often than not the centre of attention is a natural ancient woodland, a pond, an animal or even a plant. Very rarely, if ever, is it something as mundane as a shop! Sadly we have neglected to notice the imperceptible 'passing' of these once revered and treasured 'specialist' shops in village, town and city - the grocer, fishmonger, butcher and baker. They provided a personal service and quality of produce second to none - and you could choose exactly which freshly dug carrots, beans and potatoes you wished to purchase.

There is still a premium today on personal service and home grown and cooked produce - fresh local bread, home cured hams, beef slaughtered on the premises and highly flavoured local apples, plums and pears. The car and supermarket alongside mass produced cheap food on the back of vast farm subsidies and an ultra competitive market will finally seal the fate of these fascinating little shops. Many say they cannot afford to pay or choose not to pay what they see as inflated prices for produce when it is noticeably cheaper at the supermarket. It's all under one roof and there is a vast choice assembled from across the world so why bother going anywhere else when you can pile the car up with all you need for the oncoming gastronomic binge from one mega store? Convenience shopping has arrived and we all appear to have accepted it without a whimper.

I have lived in enough small market towns and villages to experience at first hand the devastating losses amongst small shopkeepers. Whatever happened to those wonderful Fen carrots complete with emerald green tops and jet black soil? It's not that long ago I saw them being loaded into crates in the fields near my home village ready for delivery to greengrocers up and down the length of the land. Potatoes and celery, like carrots, have gone the same way - washed, squeaky clean and plastic shrink wrapped to imply 'fresh' and 'infection free' to the eager waiting housewife. In truth this is not the case- they certainly taste like ' nothing on earth' and resemble a piece of chewy coloured leather. Food poisoning in its many guises has increased beyond belief and caused devastating problems to a confused and worried population. The cry goes up

'Why all this when we can buy clean and packaged food from our local supermarket'?

The complete and scientific reasons even if they were fully known would, if explained to the general public, appear complex and highly involved - good enough reason for any politician to avoid either making comment or becoming embroiled in potentially damaging discussions if they valued retaining their seat at the next election. Perish the thought! Producing and marketing shrink wrapped meat, fish and vegetables may not appear on the surface to be a likely cause of our problems but strange as it may seem it goes a long way to unravelling the mystery. 'A little bit of dirt did no-one any harm'- whoever can take the credit for this quotation was far closer to the truth than we probably realise.

In the small Fenland market town of Whittlesey where we bought our first cottage there was a delightful grocery and delicatessen. Len and his wife Marjorie had run their business for many years without the burden of endless legislation covering food hygiene yet no one had apparently suffered any ill effects from their glorious selection of specialist foods. Like Arkwright in the BBC comedy 'Open all hours' they employed an errand boy complete with a genuine 'steed' which was parked proudly outside the shop on the public footpath no less, ready for action; 'Granville', I presumed, complete with cycle clips, prepared the boxes of groceries in the room behind the shop ready for loading onto the bicycle and the inevitable perilous journey around the town's streets. Heaven forbid the present authorities would allow such follies! Neither Len or my uncle, who ran a similar establishment in Cheltenham, called St. Anne's Dairy, would ever be allowed to provide such a personal service these days - the local authority and the European Commission would ensure it did not meet the standards pertaining to the 'purveyance of groceries'. The spoilsports!

Len and his wife retired some time ago but with no one interested in devoting their life to this dying trade his grocers emporium closed it's doors forever. Our local butcher and baker suffered similar fates but in their case it was more at the hands of unsustainable costs in meeting new and crippling European legislation. No more does the smell of freshly baked bread waft across the market square and the butchers shop close to St. Andrews Church, where home slaughtered beef graced the shelves and counter, is now an Estate Agents! How our towns and villages have become impoverished. What have we gained in some 30 years whilst the spreading supermarket has cast its tentacles across town and village alike? Nothing! But we have lost an awful lot! Once a nation of shopkeepers we have become nothing more than individuals with no community spirit or sense of place save for ensuring that we survive at the expense of everyone else. Some, I believe, call this the free market economy - I would rather call it a 'free for all' which is eroding the very backbone of the country at an alarming rate.

Even the milk delivery rounds men and the famous British 'pinta' in glass bottles no less is seriously under threat. The horse and cart deliveries ceased to be some 40 years ago and the Coop bread rounds, although converted to electric floats like their 'milk cousins', followed into oblivion very soon after. When I was desperate for money I became a bread rounds man for the Coop in Whittlesey delivering bread, cakes and fancies to customers in my 'up market' electric float. It was not a job to be recommended. Necessity demanded you rose before the sun had even considered getting out of bed and wet weather brought all manner of nightmares - not least keeping your 'fancies' from getting wet! Woe betide you on your return to the depot if you had allowed as much as a drop to despoil and contaminate the goods and you were a penny out with your takings! My only other fear was for the poor unfortunate van to lose power on a slight incline and grind to a halt - something they were prone to do particularly when traffic was already queuing up behind. If the government had their way even the friendly postman and his deliveries, an underrated social contact in rural areas, will be consigned to history. The EEC also inform us now that we have the wrong shaped bananas and cucumbers. Is nothing sacred?

But I digress.

Maybe I am too hasty in overlooking that elite but fast dwindling band of small privately owned shops who still strive to bring the true British produce - be it fruit, vegetables, meat or fish - to those seemingly decreasing but most discerning customers. Many of the general public feel these people must have more money than sense but envy their ability to buy wholesome produce which is genuinely home grown. It is almost unanimously accepted that natural, organic and wholesome British food brought direct from field, river or coast now attracts a financial premium. Who is to blame for this sad state of affairs? The local fishmonger, butcher, baker and grocer have fought long and hard against the growing onslaught from rapidly improved mobility and incomes and the all pervasive supermarket that grew out of almost nothing some 30 years ago. You could quite easily be in any European country when you speed your trolley around the supermarket- it has become so standardized and anonymous. Individual shops with their personal touch and service have become a rarity so much so that they could do well to place a notice in their window reading thus -

'Endangered species - please give generously to avoid extinction'.

BADGERS AND BARN OWLS

Politicians and councillors attract deluges of criticism and hard hitting side swipes from the public and media almost every day of their life and many would say they become immune, nay thick skinned to these constant attacks.

'Why not?' say the badger and barn owl sitting in judgement.

'They should be protecting our countryside. How can we live and rear our young if you destroy the hedgerows, meadows and ponds to make way for by passes and motorways, houses and industry and the pollution they create?'

What if badgers, barn owls, hedgehogs and even sheep were our politicians and councillors and sat on Planning and Environment Committees - the countryside would be a joy to behold! Man has a supercilious high handed attitude to the environment with time to consider, plan and implement unlike the butterfly whose life is beautiful yet manifestly brief - just a single day. Yet we are pushing the wildlife to one side, re ordering, re arranging and destroying the environment to suit our needs leaving nowhere for the badgers and barn owls to go. For these and many other creatures the countryside and our back gardens is their home and habitat where they struggle to compete for survival with other animals to ensure their species in perpetuity. The balance is fine and fragile. Each thoughtless or determinedly planned change forced by man destroys another habitat and robs wildlife of its inherent privileges and right to live and raise offspring. Ask the creatures that attempt to feed, breed and roost in the hedgerows, woodland and moor land if they have an easy time.

My new next door neighbour in our West Wales village came from the affluent South East and even though he is a great 'supporter' of the local pub his ways and actions are more akin to urban man than ever rural Wales. He asked me just recently if he could bring a tractor and flail across Home Meadow so that he could remove all the 'untidy' gorse on his small patch of pasture. Thankfully, some time ago we made a decision to reduce the width of access to Home Meadow which effectively ruled out the entry of a tractor and, as I pointed out to him, the steepness of the land precluded such a suicidal mission! I was mightily relieved that our local flock of Long Tailed Tits would be safe after all. But how wrong I was, for returning one afternoon a week or so later, I was greeted with the sight and noise of a gaggle of chainsaws removing the offending gorse! The operation was thankfully quickly curtailed with the chainsaws retreating, bruised and battered, from the tough and resilient gorse wood - at least some of the gorse cover had been spared. Long Tailed Tits don't have Estate Agents but they can still use our 'managed' gorse alongside the sheep in Middle Meadow.

As my neighbour saw gorse as an unwanton intrusion on his land so man appears to regard the once common and admired hedgerows as an obstacle and inconvenience to his avowed aim of 'getting rich' at any cost. Hedge laying and coppicing, commonplace in my father's time and regarded as crucial to countryside management and the rural economy, has all but disappeared. The data produced by various countryside organisations is almost too much to bear - mile upon mile of hedge and roadside ditch lost every year. The losses seem endless; where will it all end? Local councils, despite their claims of continuing impoverishment, seem hell bent on flailing our hedgerows to extinction and replacing roadside verges and ditches, teeming with flora and fauna, by 'blacktop' and miles of underground plastic drainpipes which very rarely work. The universal excuse is predictable - road safety! Why should we encourage greater numbers of cars and giant, overloaded lorries to thunder and speed along country lanes and offer them even more opportunities to show off their prowess by widening lanes at the expense of our precious countryside? It is totally out of order!

The Local Authority and Community Council that represent our patch of the county are some of the worst culprits. Complaining bitterly of impending job losses in order to balance the budget and passing policies to promote tourism and protect the countryside, they conveniently sidestep vociferous public opinion and common sense. Meeting a stiff lipped and starchy Highways Officer one morning in our village lane I was brusquely in formed our hedgerow did not 'conform' to highway requirements; it had been the subject of complaints from the Community Council and a local haulage contractor! Apparently it wasn't the right shape, restricted views and prevented the safe passage of 30 ton lorries loaded with agricultural feed, concrete or road stone - according to him it was in the wrong place! This doyen of the establishment promptly walked back down the lane to our 1 acre wood obviously feeling that he should now press home what he thought was his advantage. Critically eyeing the ancient oak and ash which overhung the lane he launched himself into a diatribe about these poor unfortunate trees. They did not meet the 'standard' for trees bordering roads - how could I have guessed? They also fell foul of the standard clearance above the road that the authority had set in "concrete".

'There must be a minimum distance of 16 feet 6 inches between the road surface and any overhanging branches to prevent damage to vehicles using the road'.

What about damage to the trees which have a far greater pedigree than the internal combustion engines that happen to pass down our lane? Trees can be damaged but not overloaded lorries stacked like multi storey buildings with hay and straw bales! Bemused and stunned I stupidly asked the man if they in fact checked these 'magic measurements' - in an almost offensive and stilted manner he replied in the affirmative! To this day I still have visions of Highways Officers beavering around the country lanes with tapes and long poles measuring the 'magic' distance from some poor uninformed tree.

'Six inches too low ....that tree'll have to go!'

Did anyone ask the tree why had it grown thus?

Walking back to our non standard hedgerow which the family had been trying to protect for over 5 years in preparation for hedge laying I vainly tried to explain the reasons why we wished to prevent our hedge being swept away. Heaven knows we had already lost the accompanying verge and ditch a year previously when council workers moved in literally overnight and would not heed our concerns at what they were doing. Mention of hedge laying, encouraging wildlife and wildflowers and burgeoning field trees seemed to be a foreign language to the Highways Heathens - a language they either couldn't or wouldn't understand. Their 'language' appears to centre around 'arrow' straight, wide and unimaginative roads with concrete bridges and certainly no trees or hedges in sight. I have grave doubts that new legislation to protect hedges and their wildlife will have any impact in Wales as most public protagonists already openly ignore existing laws which should protect the likes of Listed Buildings and the minor parts of the built heritage. As for my 'out of touch' Highways Officer, like others, he will, I'm sure remain sublimely indifferent and use road safety as always as the excuse for spreading mayhem across the countryside.

Hedge laying and coppicing are, we are told, enjoying something of a revival but for many creatures reliant on the habitats it is too late. The For Sale notice which appeared some years ago has now been replaced by new signs warning 'Danger - Inconvenient hedge' and the sounds of the approaching yellow bellied JCB!

Our countryside and environment are a precious commodity ' on loan ' to us during our allotted span on this earth. We can easily destroy what has taken thousands of years to develop but we also have the power to support and conserve. The badger and the barn owl and their many country friends cannot manage hedgerows and woodland nor care for and graze meadows and moor land and plant trees to replace those mindlessly removed - only man can. Wildlife is pretty disgusted at intensive farming and even more so at the hideous developments quaintly termed as 'environmentally friendly'. Friendly to whom? The bank manager?

Our world will sorely be diminished if we ignore what the 'Planning Committee' say - the wildlife and countryside are essential to man's well being and happiness.

Perhaps one day the badger and barn owl will sit in final judgement.

Disregard them at our peril!

Footnote: August 2006. We have had a further two contacts from the Highways Officer – now renamed the "Street Scene" Officer – concerning our offending trees. This time they seem reluctant to meet me in person in the lane, but rather send me bureaucratic and jargon-laden letters. Interestingly, about a month ago on my return from Weston-super-Mare I found my way blocked in the lane near the farmhouse – a lorry well over-laden in height with straw had tipped over after colliding with trees. The branches in question were well over the 'magic' 16 feet 6 inch clearance!!

NOTHING TO DO WITH US 'GUV

I was sitting quietly with my father the other day on the old garden seat soaking up the warm June sunshine and passing the time on various pertinent topics when the peace was suddenly shattered. The County Council Highways men had appeared, as if from nowhere, complete with road roller and large tipper lorry to lay some stone chippings on the lane. The cacophony that ensued was beyond belief and the resultant damage even harder to accept.

Ever since we moved to West Wales we have fought a running battle with the Highways Department whether it be over our precious ancient hedgerow and its accompanying field trees or the speed at which vehicles 'burn rubber' coming into the village. I am told with great authority that Highways are all powerful and cannot be countermanded whilst at the same time they conveniently claim to have no control over speeding vehicles in our narrow, winding country lanes. There must be a special madness afflicting this section of the local authority as they have been implementing a vast programme in the locality, and no doubt throughout the county, of removing roadside ditches and verges with impunity in the interests of road safety no less! The result - vehicles travel faster! Even the highways men accept this.

I remember many years ago whilst living in Peterborough that a particular local Methodist Chapel in our city that was placed, some would say strategically in religious terms, on the very point of a sharp corner of a trunk road fell victim to the bureaucratic machinery. I have come across far more serious corners than this but for some inexplicable reason it continually caused mayhem and destruction. The 'end of the road' was literally reached one day when a young motorcyclist wrapped himself and his machine around a lamppost and then finally demolished the chapel boundary wall. Despite all the evidence accumulated over many years and the protestations of the Chapel Trustees and nearby residents who lived in fear of their lives the authorities would not even consider signing the corner as dangerous. At one point a policeman noted with some poignancy that the road could not be classified as 'dangerous' since insufficient accidents and fatalities had been reported! To this day the corner remains unsigned although the Chapel and several neighbours have ceased to reconstruct their boundary walls. No doubt, and not surprisingly, they are fed up with rebuilding them every few months since their insurance companies have refused to repeatedly 'cough up'.

Whether at local, regional or national level there is a worrying malaise in public authorities and organisations none more than in my tangle with the Highways men. Reactions to my concerns that their machinery was damaging many of our trees and that they had secured two large road signs to one of our mature sycamores by 6 inch nails ranged from indifference and total disdain to foul language. Where was their duty of care to property and the supposed promotion of an understanding image by the local authority? Where was the pride in their job?

It matters little today whether it be the Highways or Planning Departments you are in conflict with or that you care deeply about the much wider issue of the social divide between rich and poor and urban and rural communities, often 'created' by our beloved Members of Parliament, as few of these august bodies truly care. Despite their protestations our political masters have little thought or consideration to the fate of the 'people' and the 'nation' and they are certainly experts at avoiding answering any questions on awkward and delicate subjects. Presumably this is an essential in anyone's curriculum vitae when aspiring to be a politician at any level. Tough words - but there is more than an element of truth in it!

'You can't legislate against this' some wise old sage once told me. 'Politicians and leaders of every 'colour' and persuasion have a lot to answer for - they just provide the bullets and others fire the gun. Convenient isn't it? Just make sure your children grow up to respect everything and everyone in society - they all have a place'.

Reflecting on my old friends words I felt not just anger but sadness at the reaction of the council workman after I had confronted him with the damage caused to the trees. As he turned away and shovelled another load of chippings he mumbled

'Nothing to do with us 'guv'.

HIGH AND MIGHTY
(THE LORD MOVES IN A
MYSTERIOUS WAY)

There is nothing more awkward than being assailed by a fully committed, handbag waving Welsh lady just as I thought I had managed to escape from the village church having already glad handed many of the church faithful and, of course the vicar, and promised to find time to investigate a possible clom cottage in the nearby parish. I was finally 'pinned down' near the lychgate, and despite the continued passage of the children keen to reach home and prepare for Christmas, the dear lady let forth in a diatribe about the very building in which we had pleasurably enjoyed the carol service. Her final words, for at that point she set off in search of her offspring, still ring in my ears today. 'The church has moved!'

I was so taken aback by this statement that I must have returned up the village street to the farmhouse in a state of shock - I certainly don't remember walking up the hill past the old vicarage and the council houses. As if to reinforce this almost heavenly message our youngest son burst into the kitchen clutching the end of term paraphernalia and blurted out 'Dad - did you know the church has moved?' Not another one! It must be official I thought.

Church moving is not that uncommon if you think carefully around the subject. Most, if not all of our ancient religious buildings have 'moved' within the same site over many generations as new stalwarts and benefactors decided to rebuild or extend their churches with new found wealth based off the 'fat of the land'. The Cotswolds, a centre and hub of tourism attracting people from all walks of life and from across the world, is no exception. The celebrated Cotswold tradition and character developed and enhanced on the back of a once thriving woollen industry, and admired throughout the world as so atypically English, is as much under threat of obliteration as that of the once all providing famous Cotswold sheep or 'Lion' as it was once known. So important was the Cotswold woollen trade for the whole country, being a major industry even by today's standards, that the Lord Chancellor in Parliament took the 'woolsack' of Cotswold wool as his traditional seat. The churches, mansions and humble cottages reflect a rich, diverse and once thriving district whether it be in the grand Roman centre of Cirencester with it's high and mighty parish church, the proud towns of Tetbury, Broadway, and Chipping Campden or the tight knit communities of the Tews, Swells and the Slaughters. And yet in spite of all the glamour and attention that the Cotswolds receives it's way of life and unique buildings are balanced on a knife - edge and the storm clouds are gathering. The invasion of mass - produced modern materials, modern building techniques and almost ironically, greater wealth, is rapidly pushing back the boundaries between the mundane everyday towns and villages across the country and the quintessential Cotswold character. Brave efforts by Conservation Officers and forward thinking Buildings Trusts have helped stem the tide but when a modern residential development 'tarted up' in local materials appears in the very village whose main resident is none other than the current heir to the throne one really wonders if the cause is well and truly lost!

With this threat however comes a potentially far more catastrophic disaster - the complete breakdown of whole communities until, quite recently, still centred around village and town centres where residents lived, worked, raised families and bought their needs locally every day of the year. 'Going' or 'gone' are the village businesses, craftsmen and farmers and in their place has come a new 'breed' of highly mobile, well paid, transient and esoteric beings; they frequently bring with them hardly any sense of community spirit, little or no reliance on local businesses and certainly little desire to live and work in and with the community. This 'cloned ' being would far rather commute to Oxford, Birmingham or the 'big smoke'. In it's wake it is quite happy to bring along a rag tag of unwanted urban sprawl and hideous mass production bungalows and houses to blight and ruin untainted village scenes - then be even happier to call it an 'improvement'. Hidden beneath the still outward show of quality and well manicured villages, where miraculously fetes and local football, cricket and darts manage to survive albeit around a much modernised and customised 'theme' pub, is another rapidly developing problem. The village youth, the lifeblood of the future, are deserting the countryside in droves. Where once they could rely on local employment whether it be with the large Estate, the builder, stonemason, plumber, farrier or undertaker, the shop or post office or even on their own parent's farm, this is now a receding reality. The large Estate and the local farms no longer need to employ on the scale once so common whilst the local tradesmen and the village shop have quite frequently been forced out of business and their premises, now considered as quaint and unusual, taken over by the incoming urban rich! Even finding reasonably well paid employment in the nearest town, often some 15-20 miles distant, has not proved to be the answer. Only too often their home village has been virtually overrun and bought out by the high flying long distance commuters whose purchasing power has dispelled any hopes that local youngsters could afford to buy their own property. Faced with an intractable problem the youth are now setting their sights higher and moving away permanently to towns and cities.

Things are not right in the countryside. Villages, once the hub of intensive community life are, to all intents and purposes 'dead' during most of the week and even rarely spark to life at the weekends. Working for one of the Cotswold local authorities recently I discovered and experienced at first hand this very phenomenon . It seemed to matter little whether it was a baking hot summers day or raining 'stair rods' as nothing moved from dawn to dusk. Whatever malaise was befalling these villages it might as well have been a permanent siesta! Few either seem willing or able to halt this slide into oblivion. Maybe we should let history takes it's cyclical course as ever and allow villages and communities to become 'deserted' as in the Middle Ages rather than let them limp on as mere shells of their former glory. Perhaps we would then find that the 'village' would move and relocate to a site more suited to the economic climate and demands of the 21st. century.

But how could we forget the expected invasion of tourists? It is quite conceivable that a new breed of tourist would develop that admired the newly moved community with its 'could be anywhere' anonymous house and bungalows awash with UPVC windows and doors! If the present apparent impasse in the countryside is not addressed swiftly there will be nowhere for the tourists to go at all and any remote thoughts of some salvation even from the cheque books and purses of these holidaymakers will be lost forever. What is certain is that we all need to radically rethink our conception of the village and town and adapt to using the modern technology that is now all around us. As we enter the new millennium we cannot afford to allow our countryside to be 'pickled' and hope it will survive everything that is thrown at it. The telecottage could well be the answer - a technology base with computers, TV, Teletext and a fax machine - in fact everything which would function as a training centre, library, electronic post office and communications workshop as well, and probably most importantly, as a social meeting place. It may not be the total answer to the dilemma nor may it yet be the bitterest pill that many born and bred country folk will have to swallow if their beloved land is to survive in anything like it's present form. Village workshops and offices integrated within small scale, sensitive vernacular housing could well be the norm for our villages of the future. Fancy working from home rather than be faced with the battle to reach some grim, unforbidding, monolithic, multi storey office block by car! Just think of the benefits to the community and the environment - and your own sanity! Villages would live again and our air across the whole nation would be healthier and cleaner.

Somehow I cannot see the dear lady in our village accepting the modern concept of rural communities along with its communal computers and fax machines. For years to come she will still be wandering around the village muttering 'The church has moved'.

Maybe it has and it will be for the best - so be it.

The Lord moves in a mysterious way!

GATHERING CLOUDS

Sir Nikolaus Pevsner aptly described vernacular architecture as having the same 'conscious aesthetic intention' as any fine building but with a little something far more important - they belonged to the district where they were found and nowhere else.

The vernacular has much in common with language. It is not polite speech yet it is not offensive. It is local like a dialect but is certainly not abusive. These often unsung buildings reflect the simple demands of family life and farming ways using traditional designs and built of materials close to hand. They are true down to earth home cooking and a preference for them is not nostalgia but rather a desire for what is better and permanent allowing ourselves not to be subjugated to junk building - which is to all intents and purposes instantly disposable! Heaven knows we are already knocking down the mistakes and decaying buildings of just 30 years ago!

A close colleague once remarked on how our 300 year old Welsh farmhouse had apparently stood the test of time relatively unscathed whilst her recent acquisition, a 'fast track' 8 year old house was literally 'cracking up'. She had become quite accustomed to viewing the ever widening cracks in wall and ceiling plaster but decided enough was enough when she found herself eating as much plaster as breakfast cereal at the kitchen table. As with many modern buildings there are no easy answers which my colleague was to find out to her cost.

'Of course' my Structural Engineer cautiously said 'If this were a really old brick or stone house we could give you an answer to your problem straightaway. This modern multi material trash just isn't built to last - it has no guts or character - it's just disposable like so many other things these days'.

Still my friend pressed me for an answer to what was no doubt to her a very serious question. It seemed to demand a philosophical rather than a technical response and if I were honest there was no straightforward answer to the woes afflicting her poor building.

'Today's builders no longer have the essential ingredients of local knowledge, harmony and affinity with the land, it's people and resources.' I told her. Not intending to be hurtful I added for good measure that few appreciate modern houses only have an official expected lifespan of 60 years. 'My old farmhouse in Wales, like many other ancient houses, were organically grown rather like home grown potatoes and runner beans - there's nothing to beat them!'

My friend was shocked but I could tell not totally surprised. Working for some years alongside those stalwarts and faithful guardians of the built heritage, Building Preservation Trusts, she had seen at first hand how ancient buildings seem to have the sheer tenacity and will to survive whatever is thrown at them. My Engineer and I had no easy solutions to her problems but one word of advice - invest in a truly vernacular mud cottage and you won't go far wrong!

Like it or not modern buildings and structures invade every day of our life whether it be in our own locality or when we travel further afield. The celebrations that surrounded the opening of the second Severn Crossing and the eloquence of the 'great and good' extolling the new opportunities for Wales to secure a greater chunk of inward investment still ring in my ears. I am still bemused as to why politicians and the public need to persuade us that two bridges rather than one will bring us more prosperity and wealth, and much needed jobs, at the expense of our rightly admired landscape and vanishing heritage. Am I missing something? What is the price of progress? It is almost as if we fear being left behind. But how can we display our unique cultural heritage which the new European regionalism favours if it has already been eroded, either being torn down to be replaced by tawdry, low value standardised development or just left uncaringly and indifferently to decay? The national response in the principality to these home truths is only too often an almost unanimous, defensive attitude and affront, defiantly declaring that we are 'Welsh' and have our own language! In all the frantic emotions surrounding the declaration of 'Welshness' the vernacular goes unnoticed - if only our fellow citizens could but observe and understand the true culture. Rhetoric will not save Welsh Wales!

According to writer Jan Morris, whether in the foothills of Snowdonia, the green heartland of the Borders or the soft pastoral landscape of the South West, the Welsh 'possess a conciliating power and ability to unite structure with it's setting and make it feel part of nature'. This is still true in a few isolated places but they are growing fewer by the day. Many of our vernacular buildings face permanent mutilation and, in many cases, total destruction effected with complete impunity and indifference; and my county is one of the worst offenders and sufferers! The humble cottage and barn are delicate and fragile pieces of history - they are not just a 'pile of stones' but rather a slice through the Welsh heritage. Everyone is charged with its care, 'wrinkles and all', and we have no right to impose our authority on it's character. We are all guardians of our past for the future, a responsibility we seem only too eager to avoid. Be it at our peril!

How could I ever fail to remember the day I met an old Welsh farmer leading an aged ram on a length of rope down a narrow country lane. I was unable yet unwilling to rush this obviously important event as he (and the ram) seemed quite oblivious to my presence until turning into a farm gateway the old gentleman slowly looked round and mumbled 'Bore da' as I wound down the car window. I was in luck this time - it was one of the few Welsh phrases I understood! But I had no need to worry as my eldest son, fluent in Welsh, was sitting next to me. Protracted talk ensued with my son acting as an interpreter and it soon became clear this very farmer was the owner of a building we were searching for. Initial hostility gradually gave way to scepticism and eventual curiosity - what on earth was an Englishman doing in the middle of the Welsh countryside looking for a dilapidated building which could only be described as a terminal case? He once more became very concerned and I started to recognise worrying phrases such as Inland Revenue and Local Authority. I quickly calmed him by totally disassociating myself from these worthy but to many, all too intrusive bodies and thus relieved, the conversation flowed once more. We left him, still holding the ram, thanking him profusely in Welsh and English and clutching the camera in the sure knowledge we had a record of the ancient building on film - possibly the last sighting! My son later recounted to me the essence of the farmer's last few words - apparently he had only bought the decaying building to prevent anyone else living next door! It seemed he had no intention of repairing it for himself or for farm use and couldn't understand what I saw in a heap of old rubble! His last words were that he might well back the tractor into it once we had left! My heart sank at the thought of this unthinking action on such a fine example of the Welsh vernacular which even in its last throws epitomised the culture of rural Welsh life. I have never dared go back!

Many panic at the thought of retaining the 'history' of a building fearing that it means 'living in the past' and returning to cooking cawl on an open fire, using oil lamps, fetching water from a well or paying a hurried visit in the middle of the night to the ty bach at the bottom of the garden. As Martin Davies, a local advocate and supporter of the vernacular, so aptly put it

'You would never dream of 'putting a digital face on a grandfather clock'.

But this is exactly what Wales has perpetrated on it's fast dwindling stock of vernacular buildings for as many years as anyone can recall - and it has produced the most bizarre and horrific hybrids - certainly not welcome additions to the landscape. A little sacrifice can go a long way and with care, sympathy and humility, modern requirements, other than UPVC, can usually be accommodated without pushing these vulnerable ancient buildings over the brink and beyond recall. Their hold on life may be tenacious but there is no doubt their future is precarious!

I have often been branded a 'wild visionary' and 'romantic' and of being far too easily led by my emotions. But whilst humble cottages and farm buildings lie abandoned in ruins with remnants of once proud structures standing like ghosts against a leaden, rain soaked sky I am drawn to believe that we have all been missing the very essence of the 'emotion' fired by the community spirit that created these buildings. Rather, we have vainly searched for some bold, imaginative and impressive architectural statement which will never be found amidst the dying embers rapidly being overtaken by nature. Separation, deliberately or by wanton neglect, of native language, folk culture and landscape will, in time, mean total failure. Each relies on one another for their continuance and cannot stand alone. Our greed for a 'bit of everything' that everyone else has without thought of the consequences will inevitably lead to the disembowelment of whole communities, their spirit, folklore and traditions - even with the promise of 'jam today ...and tomorrow' from the European Community! The Welsh vernacular provides a fertile organic enrichment yet is unsophisticated but honest in its unpretentious character. What little remains is memorable and vividly displays the true heart and soul of Welsh culture and rural life. It is truly magical and ethereal and there is little that can match it in the kingdom. Sadly it lies in tatters, a mere shadow of it's past - the principality's most prized asset is in its twilight years. Under lowering grey skies the end is close at hand.

I rest my case.

NOW AND FOREVER

The notice on the county boundary is stark and to the point –

'No room - this County is full!'

This is not a joke but reality. It's one thing to put a 'Full' notice at the entrance to a National Park during peak holiday time knowing many visitors will return home at light fall but it is deadly serious when the notice goes up in an English county.

A dear old lady, who had lived in a delightful village for almost the whole of her life, said to me 'These people just keep arriving - I've nothing against them and their wish to live here but how will the community cope? Looking out of her cottage that once stood on the very edge of the village surrounded by meadow, farmsteads and hayricks - and is now an ugly executive housing estate - she made a hard hitting statement.

'There's just no room for anymore people'.

People have to live somewhere, but she did have a point.

With some 56million souls attempting to live on 56million acres we are fast becoming a very crowded island - some would go as far as to say overcrowded. Logically, and with all things being equal, this would mean we each would have an acre of land, but as many know, including our beloved parliamentarians, this is just not the case. Long gone are the days when everyone could own an acre plus a cow, a pig and a sheep - most families are lucky to have a garden equivalent to just one twentieth of an acre!

It doesn't take long to recognise on a tour of villages and small towns across the breadth of the country that we are running out of 'new land' to develop - it just doesn't exist! The only change is in our use of existing land. Too long have we assumed that 'green field' sites should be used for development - what about recycling land that has been used once, twice or even 3 times before? Let's not deny people the joys of living in the 'country' but be sure to prevent suburbia overtaking the precious countryside. Errors a plenty have been perpetrated since the Industrial Revolution evolved over 3 centuries ago and we should take the lead in cleaning up this mess - not adding to it for future generations. Strangely to many - and these include estate agents, developers and the government - more people are rediscovering city and town dwelling and it's pleasures. Developers, Estate agents and the population of this tiny island have a lot to answer for - the agent's typical reaction to selling 'up market' houses on an ancient meadow in the heart of an unspoilt village is simply: 'It's a desirable place!' This cannot be a satisfactory answer. Are we all that short sighted and uncaring about our very own country? Sadly the answer is 'yes'. Only too often I despair at the attitude of the 'man in the street' and some would say little wonder when you look at politicians at national or local level - they hardly give a good image or lead by example!

We may have failed to address errors in times past but this cannot give us the right to blindly follow the same disastrous path like sheep. Surely we should have learnt our lesson by now? Our Prehistoric and Roman ancestors practised the very discipline we should be promoting in the 21st.century - time and time again they reused their ancient sites even when they didn't have the pressure of 56million people living on 56million acres! These were the 'brown field' sites of ancient history and the archaeologists can prove it!

Brian Redhead, that well read author and much loved broadcaster, once said

'We need city life to prove that we are civilised and we need country to prove that we are whole'.

How true.

We all need to be assured that the countryside is safe, cared for and not plundered - now and forever!

Footnote: August 2006. We are now told the population has grown to 60 million! The country is certainly overcrowded! The present Government still insists that thousands of new properties will be built on Green Belt, whilst the opposition don't seem to offer any alternatives. We shall soon run out of open countryside just to walk the dog!

A ty bach near Cwmdu, Carmarthenshire

Farmhouse and Llanfynydd
viewed from
Top Meadow

Honeyway Cottage,
Whittlesey in 1979
ahead of restoration

Llwyn Haf, Cwrt Henri, Carmarthenshire - mud cottage with tin over thatch

*Decaying Vernacular - Blaen-Nant-Gwyn,
Mynydd Llanfihangel Rhos y Corn, Carmarthenshire*

The Old Cobblers Shop, Llanfynydd

The Weir, Warboys

Young boys fishing on the Weir, Warboys

Timber and mud firehood at Honeyway Cottage, Whittlesey

*Inglenook at Honeyway Cottage, Whittlesey
where 'superstitious chickens' were found*

Gorse on our land in Wales - home of the Long Tailed Tit

Tray loaded with grapes from St. Egwad's Vineyard, Llanfynydd

View from Middle Meadow of St. Egwad's Vineyard and farmhouse, Llanfynydd

VI

IT'S
A
MAD MAD WORLD

WITCHES AND WARLOCKS

My old home village would to many seem nothing special - just a large Fenland settlement dominated by a fine parish church, a substantial pyramidal roofed Jubilee clock tower and blessed with an enormous pond called the Weir. This was the very pond where my grandfather used to regularly call to load up with water before leading the horse drawn cart back down into the dank fens whereupon water (and frogs) were decanted for family use. I have never been told what happened to the poor hapless frogs that became caught up in this ritual; presumably they leapt to safety into one of the many reed filled dykes!

But the village hides a much darker and sinister past than any present day passer by could ever imagine - in fact a past so awesome that the events which took place some 400 years ago are recorded as one of the most notorious trials in the whole sordid history of English witch hunting! It was common practice in those days for the village pond to be the scene of many an attempt by credulous villagers to 'convict' with the flimsiest of evidence any 'misfit' or older women, often living alone with a cat for companionship, as witches. Ducking stools were regularly used to publicly humiliate likely candidates but even more unjust was the practice of 'swimming' the victims in a local river or stream to observe whether they floated or sank. To put it bluntly it was a ' no win' situation - if the victim floated they were immediately seized as being a witch and hung and if they sank they just drowned!

The worst possible scenario occurred in my old village of Warboys where witches began in the vivid imagination of a 10 year old sick child and ended in the violent deaths of 3 innocent people. As was so often the case it was all too easy for a prosperous country family supported by their gullible physician to place suspicion on a simple uneducated country person. Apparently bewitched by 'evil spirits' the 4 daughters of the family fell ill with prolonged sneezing bouts and fits which suspiciously became worse in the presence of strangers whilst none other than Lady Cromwell dreamt of being attacked by a cat sent by the witch, took ill and died some months later.

The daughter's family pestered the hapless victim into confession persuading her to cast out the evil spirits and all seemed happier until the old lady retracted everything. Arrested on the order of the family she became half demented. Along with her husband and daughter who were conveniently implicated they were all found guilty of bewitching and causing Lady Cromwell's death by sorcery. Victims of mischievous children and the credulity of their elders all three were hanged at the Local Assizes in 1593. Sad as these events may be it still remains a mystery as to why the village have never recorded or honoured these happenings considered at the time as of extreme national importance. Who knows there could still be descendants of the most unfortunate people living in the village or within the fenland community nearby.

It is however little wonder that some businessmen would latch onto the murky history of the village and exploit it, if that is the right phrase. I readily remember the sight of the cream and blue buses belonging to the village omnibus company either parked neatly outside their garage or wending their way down the main street resplendent with a witch on a broomstick as a logo. Even the village football team now use the very same motif on their shirts!

The village now goes about its usual business. I would imagine that many of the newcomers in the recently built sprawling estate near the Clock Tower have little idea or inkling of what took place 400 years ago. The cream and blue buses are long since gone along with their vivid reminder and there is nothing at the pond but just a few goldfish no doubt left over from the Feast Day and, of course, a few frogs! On the bank are some youngsters trying their hand at fishing.

All is now peace.

Footnote: I recently met two local lads, Jo and Albert, having great success fishing on the Weir. They were regularly hauling in sizeable carp and perch and were so proud of their catches which they reverently returned to the Weir.

SUPERSTITIOUS CHICKENS

The last thing you expect to find holed up in the side of an inglenook fireplace is a chicken - albeit long since dead, but definitely a chicken! There is little doubt it was a free range bird and certainly not one of those factory reared versions. Until it met it's fate in the side of our fireplace it must have led a contented life scratching around for morsels in the farmyard.

Back in the heady days of 1979 we had fallen upon a neglected, unloved tiny cottage complete with tin roof and a lean - to privy, tucked away down a narrow track quaintly called Finkle Lane in the Fenland market town of Whittlesey. Little did we realise the 'adventure' upon which we were embarking since we were both convinced, even before struggling through the overgrown garden, soon to be named the Amazon jungle, that we were destined to own this forlorn building. The agents vividly described the cottage as 'ripe for renovation'. Nature had truly overtaken what little remained of the old farmyard which had been divided up and adapted as a garden probably some 100 years previously; inch thick Russian Vine and life threatening briars penetrated through windows and doors, around the chimney and under the roof! Unsure of what to expect, and certainly not a chicken, we entered a time warp accompanied by the Estate Agent, an elderly fat gentleman who resembled Mr Bumble from Charles Dicken's 'Oliver'. The cottage was so tiny that it took but a few minutes to view the accommodation; the fat gentleman continually muttered 'it's as dry as a bone' and 'all it needs is capping' - it was as if he were a continuous playing tape! As so often in these situations, despite it being our first 'dive' into the property market, nostalgia overtook us. Surely the agent should have been repeating 'beware - this building has every known problem including dead chickens!'- and why didn't he explain about the ominous rising damp and those giant woodworm?

We bought the cottage, wrinkles and all, for the princely sum of £3750!

Little did we know that we had become the proud owners of a 17th. Century gem with many endearing and unique features- not least its pint size nature but also it's fine timber framed and mud firehood that had concealed secrets for many generations. Even after 4 years of labouring to repair the building and a further 4 years living in it when we came to sell with heavy heart we were still unable to decide with any certainty it's original use. A vernacular building, born out of local skills and materials, it possessed a 'warm spirit' yet still hid deep secrets of past occupants.

Superstition and folklore lay at the heart of rural life from the very moment man discovered fire. We may not openly flaunt it but even today many have superstitions and traditions that they rigidly keep to in the belief it will bring them success, wealth and good fortune. Some even carry this, probably without realising it into seeking millions from the National Lottery. Rural man relied heavily and openly on age old traditions which were passed from generation to generation as a matter of course - they had no reason to doubt their use or validity. In the days when there was no Common Agricultural Policy to intervene, buy up unwanted surpluses or support in time of need, the farmer and smallholder had little choice but to appeal to his maker. The fire in the inglenook still represented 'life' and was rarely, if ever, allowed to go out in fear that catastrophic events would overwhelm the household. Celtic traditions went even further - cows in the byre had to be kept in full view of the hearth to ensure they would continue to produce milk whilst the fires' cleansing powers would keep them free from evil spirits and other ills.

Our 'adventure' at Honeyway Cottage, as it became known, inadvertently uncovered a tradition and superstition which had been at the centre of Fen life for many hundreds of years - a ritual that would bring fertility, good fortune and successful crops. Along with the chicken came 4 generations of worn out shoes and a sundry collection of agricultural ironmongery including gate latches and hinges. It appeared that the 'practice' had begun, at least in this fireplace, in the early 18th. Century and continued until about 1820 when the last shoe reverently placed by the 'fire' was a fine ladies slipper with a pink silk bow. We should not deride and scoff at this practice in the light of our own superstitions, however trivial we might think they are. Today, in our disposable age and consumer driven society we don't consider throwing out a pair of worn out shoes to be anything other than normal behaviour but to those living just 150 years ago that act would have been sacrilege. To ensure continuance of this tradition we placed 2 pairs of worn out shoes in the very same spot in the inglenook wall - maybe even we felt a need to appease the gods and secure a happy and fruitful stay in the cottage! The much needed but little thought of shoe retains a 'presence' of the person like nothing else - it should certainly make you think when you next sit poised on the edge of a seat about to decant socks or tights from tired and weary feet!

Kentucky fried chicken and Clark's shoes seem mighty strange bedfellows and highly unlikely candidates for being subjects of superstition - there's just no accounting for taste!

SAINTS ALIVE

Doctor's surgeries are contemplative places particularly when you are the only one left in the waiting room following the exit of what seems to be hoards of screaming and snivelling children intent, it would appear, on ensuring you, the doctor and all the staff have a flu ridden Christmas.

The surgery, as you would expect, is festooned with the usual Christmas regalia of paper chains, tinsel and the ubiquitous stable scene balanced precariously on the edge of the counter. Apart from the expected range of magazines, which, by their dog-eared state appear to have been chewed over by anxious parents for many months and now lie scattered to the four winds, close to the pharmacy is a small display box stuffed with copies of Llais y Llan, the Parish Magazine. I should admit now that this would not be my normal choice of reading material in a doctor's surgery or in fact at any time, but being frustrated at waiting, I flicked through the pages with little interest or hope that I would alight on some gem of literary discourse. How wrong I was! Never underestimate the 'Voice of the Church' or 'Llais y Llan' as it is in the Celtic tongue.

I was horror struck by a paragraph of the Vicar's Newsletter in which he chastised his 'flock', but in particular the children, over the indulgence, enjoyment and celebration of Halloween. Halloween he wrote '...is not a Christian celebration; it is not healthy and it is not harmless! It can lead to all sorts of demonic evils as more and more people see no harm in allowing their children to take part in collecting sweets and money from neighbouring houses under threat of something nasty if they don't comply. Let us protect our children from his (the devil's) influence by every means possible!'

Saints alive!

Of course Halloween is a pagan tradition as are so many of the so called Christian events and festivals which the church worldwide and it's adherents readily celebrate without even a thought as to how they may have 'travelled down' to today in their present form. Rogation, Ascension, Candlemas or the Feast of the Purification of the Virgin Mary and even Christmas and it's celebrated tree all have roots in Roman Gods, pagan rites and symbolism which have been progressively hijacked by the Christian Church. The hijacking, occasionally accidental, has more often than not been a deliberate policy by the church authorities and hierarchy to stamp a label of authenticity on events over which they had little or no control in times when the Church was supposedly all powerful.

I recall as a youngster in primary school the excitement of the forthcoming Halloween when our teachers would lead us in making lanterns - cut to give the most gruesome and ghostly faces! Living in an area renowned for sugar beet growing we would scour the streets for the very largest of these vegetables that had conveniently fallen from an overloaded lorry. Our spare moments were then spent lovingly 'sculpting' and hollowing out the beet to form fearsome eyes, nose and mouth and planting a candle at its heart. The effect was quite frightening but all in good humour as many were submitted for judging in a competition to find the most awful and frightening face. Nowadays lorries are netted for reasons of safety and thus the exciting ritual has all but vanished unless of course you know a friendly sugar beet farmer. Children now turn their attention to the pumpkin, to be found on supermarket and greengrocer's shelves, and the grotesque face making seems just as successful as we attained with the humble beet. Such activities for Halloween or All Saints or All Hallows Eve, as the church knew it, are directly linked to the ancient Celtic agricultural and pastoral year - the very beginning of the pagan New Year when the Feast of Samain was celebrated. It was considered a time when natural laws were suspended, ghosts and demons roamed abroad and the spirits of the dead were believed to make a brief return to this world, whilst great fires were lit to ensure renewal of life in the earth after it's long winter sleep. Such was the significance and power of this all important day after Halloween that the early church rededicated the day, the 1st.November, to 'all saints in heaven' - All Saints Day - the church aptly named the following day All Souls Day, which was reserved for the clergy to say masses for the poor souls in purgatory. Apart from observing these 'religious' days the Vicar no doubt had 'trick or treat' in mind.

'Souling' or 'soul caking', as it is more accurately interpreted in two Cheshire villages, is a legacy of the old pagan practice of leaving out food for the dead on the two days following Halloween. The custom to this day is portrayed by children in fancy dress and blackened faces singing a jingle at every door in return for a spiced cake or money, the entourage being supported by mummers re-enacting the Soul Caking Play with a Hodening Horse that snaps it's jaws at passers by. The horse, perhaps a relic of the animal ridden by the Norse God Odin, is accompanied by the Black Prince of Paradise, who is killed by King George and resurrected by the Quack Doctor, Old Mary, Little Dairy Doubt and Beelzebub with his frying pan 'club'. Heaven forbid that I should mention that tormentor Beelzebub!

Whichever way the Vicar turns pagan symbolism surfaces through almost every church festival and event. Candlemas Day was converted by the clergy to become the Feast of the Purification of the Virgin Mary and a day to venerate child bearing. Very few realise that this 'christian' festival took the place of the Roman Festival of Febran when candles were processed through the streets and purification rites were observed by women. Not even the major event in the Christian Year - Christmas - escapes.! The nativity is celebrated on the traditional early Christian date for the birth of Christ since the real one is truly unknown. The 25th.December absorbed many pagan festivals, most held in honour of the sun's re-birth after the winter solstice, along with the day celebrating the generosity of Saint Nicholaus who miraculously dispensed gifts into people's homes when they were most needed. Saint Nicholaus was, in turn hijacked by our present Father Christmas! The traditional Christmas tree and candles both originate from the pagan Norse Yule sun worship festival with Yule logs and candles symbolising fire and light. The Christmas tree bedecked with Yule candles was welcomed into homes as it was believed to shelter woodland spirits long after all other trees had lost their leaves. If the Vicar knew that even Guy Fawkes Night on the 5th.November had not been spared being tainted with pagan rituals I wonder if he would really have the heart to stop children enjoying fireworks, bonfires and all the festive fun. Surely it would be cruel to take away the long held belief that Guy Fawkes Day truly celebrates his infamous attempt to burn down the Houses of Parliament? Considering our on going love-hate relationship with politicians many people might secretly wish that old Guy had succeeded! That the bonfire lighting celebrates the Celtic New Year and not Guy's failed plot shouldn't concern us or dampen our spirits at one of the most dismal and disheartening times of the year. We, unlike our ancestors, may not be so reliant on the land and weather for our very being and life but we do need something in the chill of winter to brighten up our often mundane working life and quicken the onset of longer, warmer days and the Spring to come.

Maybe the Vicar and the rest of his fellow clergy have an ulterior motive and are concerned to gather more into their ever dwindling 'flock' by dwelling on the sinister and dangerous evil's of the devil that lurks at every corner awaiting to ensnare the weak and unprepared! Heaven forbid that this is their design - I've witnessed enough strife, ill feeling, and downright hostility in churches to keep me going for a lifetime! Despite all the protestations far too many wars and troubles in the world are fought over all in the name of religion. Why spoil a young child's innocence and fun?

Methinks the Vicar and his friends have got this one badly wrong!

Long live Halloween and Christmas and to that matter all other festivals - long may they prosper!

Saints be praised!

GLAD TIDINGS BE UPON YOU

Brightly coloured goldfinches flit from branch to branch defiantly calling out their territory whilst one of our blackbirds and our resident robin peck amongst the leaf mould covering the frozen ground in the hope of finding some tasty morsel. A pair of magpies kick up a cacophony in one of the ash trees as a band of marauding crows whirl high above mobbing and mocking a buzzard who, lazily and apparently unconcerned, goes about the task of patrolling his 'patch'. Ravens, having decided it's time to venture home to roost, honk to one another like the plucking of a banjo. The skies fall suddenly silent as dusk gathers pace and the sheep make their biologically tuned advance up the hill to the highest point for the night. Smoke from wood fires curls lazily upwards against a deepening blood orange red sky heralding another bitterly cold night and the arrival onto the arena of one of the most loved and respected traditions of Christmastide.

A small band of hardy carol singers, wrapped up against the oncoming chill, gather around the doors of the village houses to give a lively rendition of a familiar festive time song under the glow of a flickering lantern. 'All is peace, all is quiet' as the ancient carol tells except that in city and town across the land mayhem rules supreme. Yes, it's the last week before Christmas Day but festive decorations, cards, presents and food have already been on the shelves for the last 3 months! Panic has set in as the mad lemming like rush gathers momentum - everyone from young to old stack up with all manner of goods many of which will be thrown out half eaten or unused before the end of the festive frivolities. Over indulgence, wassailing and waistline building continue unabated for day upon day only for the whole sordid procedure of stripping bare supermarket shelves to start again between Boxing Day and New Years Eve! Even after the New Year celebrations have subsided mothers still have that determined look as they advance upon the supermarket again, trolley to the fore, almost as if it were some beast they must tame. It is sound advice to avoid even approaching any supermarket or shopping complex at this mad time of year until at least the trolleys and their 'drivers' have 'burnt off' their festive frustrations. Not only should these trolley pushers display 'L' plates but so should their motorised cousins. Lunatic drivers seem hell bent on forcing you off the road in their death defying dash to pick up the turkey, a few shrivelled brussel sprouts and some wizened old satsumas that must have certainly wished they had never left Spain!

Everyone is in a daze as if driven by some mad demon. Most, I'm certain don't know why they ventured forth to shop or what they really needed to purchase. They return home weary, fed up and despairing whilst still pondering on the thought of stuffing the turkey that they fought so hard to get and the hard labour that lies ahead in the 'steaming cauldron' - the kitchen! How we look forward to the sweat, smoke and strong language that ultimately arises from the scenes of chaos and devastation on Christmas

Eve and the most blessed of days! Christmas madness is everywhere. Even the traditional holly and mistletoe does not escape the rampaging hoards intent on having everything. The holly berries all but glow from the hedgerows amidst the closing year's first hard frost that has laid down a carpet of white across the countryside. But beware, the holly thief is close at hand! Not content with a small reminder of this most famous of woodland trees many openly remove complete trees from roadside and country lane. These inconsiderate marauders probably little realise or care how long it takes for a holly tree to reach maturity and provide us with the gift of intense red berries so well told of in the famous and ancient carol. Better, if you must, do a little trimming rather than take the whole tree!

If this 'I'm alright Jack' attitude is now our Christmas then I would rather retire gracefully to the peace and quiet of our small farm and talk to our sheep, promising them a few extra sheep nuts on Christmas Day whilst exhorting them not to overdo the Christmas Fayre in consideration of lambing that is to come. There is an old saying, the provenance of which is lost in the mists of time, that links sheep, not surprisingly, with the birth of Christ in the stable - apparently all sheep should turn to face East at midnight on Christmas Eve!

I am yet to be convinced our sheep know of this but it's a delightful and sobering thought in this mad, mad world.

Glad tidings be upon you.

FRYING TONIGHT

As soon as Christmas is over there is a lemming like rush to the travel agents. Mothers, with reluctant children, jostle and claim the most eye catching, immodest swimming costume and beach wrap whilst grabbing gallons of suntan cream to prevent the sun reaching parts they are advised it shouldn't reach.

The annual charge of the 'brits' is on to see who can be first to sizzle on some far flung beach and then to return looking as if they had been charcoal grilled. Why bother worrying about the size and colour of young James' shorts or whether you packed the pills to guard against Barbarosa's revenge when you can readily 'fry' at home. At least there is no annual pilgrimage to the airport or ferry to suffer the expected ritual, carnage and mayhem inflicted by vital workers who seem to have a second sense about downing tools at the critical moment. Things are not happening at the airport and ferry as they should be and the right and proper things are not happening at home in this green and pleasant land.

How could the summers be so hot and where is all that rain we have lovingly come to expect when the schoolchildren break for their summer holidays? Someone is not playing cricket! Strange as it may seem and much against the principles of the British our climate is changing and, some would say, rapidly. It appears there is little we can immediately do but rather console ourselves that we shall have to become accustomed to drier summers, considerably higher temperatures and accepting vineyards as a new part of our landscape. Global warming, like it or not, is here to stay for a very long time until at least we can come to terms with our car and consumer durable driven avaricious lifestyle.

Locals in our West Wales village scoffed when I first planted vines on a sheltered part of our land; some even thought I was planting soft fruit. Grapes in Wales? Never! We get far too much rain - it must be a joke!

Vineyards may come and go as they have done since medieval times but this time they are here to stay with a vengeance. As is always the case when attempting to convince doubting Thomases the only answer is to offer samples of the first vintage, a flinty, medium dry white wine, as proof that this hair brained venture can succeed. Until some 10 years ago our site would have been regarded by all viticulturalists as distinctly borderline but that is certainly not the case now. Here's to Chateau St.Egwad or rather Jasper's Leap as the first vintage has been called! Working in the vineyard in recent summer months has become something of a problem - not how to avoid becoming soaked but rather restricting your dose of ultra violet. It is a serious business when even the daily weather forecasts on television offer advisory periods of exposure to the sun before you cover up and retreat - in our case, to the ice cool of our old farmhouse. As one old gentleman once wisely told me, and obviously speaking from experience 'It's a pleasure that's unforgettable - just like going from a sauna to a deep freeze!' I wonder what he knew about saunas at his age? Regularly television and radio programmes spell out the hidden dangers of over indulgence in the sun yet we are all guilty of complacency and rationalisation - we ignore the sound advice at our peril. As with most problems afflicting our country the answer is a common one - rethink your lifestyle before it is too late. At least we have the power and knowledge to implement change - pity the poor wildlife - they have to wait for us to wake up before it's too late as they don't need to travel from these shores to receive a free dose of ultra violet!

For me, I would far rather visit my friendly fish and chip shop in a little village by the Towy estuary and buy a bag of haddock and chips. At least I know the fish is freshly caught, the chips are from Pembrokeshire potatoes and the risk of my cholesterol soaring into the sky is but small in comparison to the risks and pain suffered by those 'frying tonight'.

WILL THE LAST PERSON IN WALES PLEASE TURN OUT THE LIGHT

The world has been turned on its head and no more has it been felt harder than in rural communities where life is tough enough already.

Wales has suffered particularly badly in a rapidly deepening crisis in the farming industry with farm incomes desperately near the bread line amongst many hill farmers and the low wage economy of the principality not able to withstand the most gentle or subtle of knocks. Though it is being felt across the kingdom the Welsh situation doesn't bear comparison with the relatively stable and well off farmers in Middle and Eastern England - and that is not being vindictive against what the Welsh continue to call the 'old enemy'.

As one farmer so aptly put it –

'We're all in this together whether we like it or not'.

Rural life is on the brink of extinction and the rural heritage is under threat. The present crisis could easily be likened to the rural revolt that was provoked by the Enclosure Acts almost 200 years ago and even the great depression of the 30's when not only rural but also urban uprising was the order of the day. Nothing so fiercely defiant has been seen since the stand against the Poll Tax when a government was firmly put in its place under threat of insurrection and almost certain repetition of the mob uprisings of medieval times. The green pound, BSE, subsidy reductions, rural transport (or rather the lack of it) and rising fuel costs have become the familiar war cry of farmers, community leaders and occasional opposition MP's who are ever hopeful of an early return to parliament and the 'gravy train'. It's a pretty impasse when the Chairman of the NFU cannot sell his cattle at market, not because the prices are so abysmally low but rather the protesting farmers had occupied the selling ring! With escalating chaos threatening their livelihood and that of the locally dependant small scale machinery suppliers and feed merchants what else could they do? Many of the protestors had suffered a worse fate than their illustrious chairman - some had reached the end of the line with both their banks and their own mental state and who could blame them!

As one of our local farmers remarked

'What's the point in caring for your cattle and calving them only to have to give them away at the market at a loss. I don't sees the supermarkets lowering their prices when we're getting less than it costs to rear the animals - it's even the same with sheep and milk! Why should I bother? Are they trying to torture and starve us off the land? Given a little longer and they could succeed!'

For the first time in living memory farmers have taken to the streets, marts, supermarkets, abattoirs and even ports in a vociferous attempt to have their voice heard before it is irrevocably stifled. In one recent incident the complete contents of a juggernaut were emptied into the harbour of a Welsh port as soon as beef, destined for some fast food outlet, had been identified as being other than British - such is the anger and frustration at a situation the farmer feels he is powerless to direct or control.

Across Wales community associations, parish councils and county councils and their leaders can all be heard echoing the same familiar worrying cry. As if the countryside had not already taken enough hammer blows the cost of travelling, often considerable distances from farm to mart or home to work has been progressively increased by governments in recent years in a vain and misguided attempt to control the use of the car and it's pollution of the environment. Without appearing to knock these no doubt genuine endeavours it seems little thought has been given to the effect on rural communities where public transport is a rarity. Our own village, not that remote and within 10-12 miles of two substantial towns, still only sees a single bus 6 days a week; until recently the service was but one bus on a Saturday and a Wednesday - no doubt a hangover from transporting local folk back and forth on market days. You also need a mortgage to afford the fare! The car in the countryside is not a luxury but an absolute necessity and a lifeline without which whole villages and vast tracts of land would return to wild uninhabited and desolate landscape. Together with a dramatic fall in farm incomes, whether it be beef, dairy cattle or even sheep, the alarm bells have begun to ring for many a rural holding, the majority of which before this crisis were already marginal. I am quite certain that no urban families would ever accept the miserable pittance that many of these farmers have to survive on!

The effect on the land we love would be catastrophic. Social deprivation and abandonment of land and buildings would be rife as would be unemployment, loss of village schools, churches, chapels and the local hostelry all leaving permanent scars which would take generations to heal - if ever. Added to all this is the recent catastrophe to hit the countryside - foot and mouth. This is without doubt the biggest ever blow to strike rural Britain - words cannot describe the feeling of utter desperation, devastation and isolation. It is no exaggeration to say that the on going rural crisis is already emptying the countryside of it's truly indigenous country dwellers and workers leaving it easy prey to those with a keen eye for cheap pickings. Unfortunately most of these entrepreneurial vultures do not have the country at heart but would rather use it as a 'vehicle' for commuting whilst awaiting the opportunity to make a 'quick buck' and move on. Many of these 'smash and grab' people have little or no interest in the area they have bought into and certainly no idea or understanding of what makes the countryside 'tick'. Few, if any, put anything into the community or the local economy - it's all take and no give! Let's face it - across large areas of England and Wales already once active and vibrant villages are now but lifeless shells dubiously 'pickled' and 'neatly trimmed' to present a pristine but deceptive face. The most worrying fact about all this is that the majority of people either don't notice, don't want to notice or plainly just don't care!

The writing is on the wall - the 'living countryside' is dying by progressive strangulation and it will never be the same again. All country folk ask for is understanding, a fair return for the work and goods produced and just a 'light touch' by those all pervasive civil servants within their ivory towers in London and Brussels.

Otherwise, 'Will the last person in Wales please turn out the light?'

Tulip the sheep

The 8 lane A1(M) at Norman Cross, Peterborough

Derelict Clyn Llydan in the Cothi Valley, Carmarthenshire

Rusty Back Fern on our farmhouse

Lichens on trees on our land in Wales

*Ewe with recently
born lamb at our farmhouse*

*Monmouthshire and Brecon
Canal near Talybont on Usk*

Coed Clathen Battlefield, Broad Oak, Carmarthenshire

Trichrug, Carn Goch and Towy Valley from near Defadfa Isaf

The Mad Cat public house at Pidley near Warboys

Carew Castle, Pembrokeshire across tidal creek

Carreg Cennen Castle, The Black Mountain, Carmarthenshire

*Cadge and Colman's Flour Mill (now demolished)
beside the River Nene, Peterborough*

VII

WILD
AND
WELCOMING

LIFE IN THE SLOW LANE

'How's the family and wonderful Wales?'

Sitting in a finely upholstered chair in a hair salon is not exactly my favourite occupation but at least I had managed to find half an hour free from a hectic day of business appointments in Peterborough, the old city in which I had been raised for most of my early years. Emilio, hair stylist and great friend, had been chosen for the task of making inroads into my mop of hair. He was convinced the relaxed living, lifestyle and clean air of West Wales caused my hair to grow at an alarming rate - far faster than those of his fellow city dwellers!

He so desperately wanted to be part of 'rural life' and if he couldn't move house to Wales he hit on the next best thing - buy an old canal narrow boat and mess about on the river and one day he might reach the principality on the ever expanding network of rivers and canals.

Each time I called at the salon for a trim he updated me on the progress of the restoration programme. As the time fast approached for completion I could see the sense of excitement and anticipation for the big day when his pride and joy would be lowered into the water and moved to it's own private moorings. Mission accomplished he sold his house and moved into his river home to enjoy a peaceful and relaxed living content in the knowledge that he could 'weigh anchor' at any time and drift up river for the day stopping off at temporary moorings to down some ale at a pleasant riverside pub. At one point he even sidelined his car and took to cycling to work from his beloved craft but traffic congestion, pollution and the idiotic actions of many drivers forced him to abandon this part of the overall plan.

After several visits to his salon Emilio began to realise how the chaos and mayhem of the city affected me and fully appreciated my wish to finish business and return as fast as possible to a land of peace and sanity. He had known little else than the 'rat race' as he was one of many second and third generation Italians whose parents and grandparents had travelled to these shores in the 50's and 60's in search of work. They inevitably found themselves working for a pittance in diabolical conditions in the brickyards, which then employed vast numbers and whose screen of chimneys surrounded the city on three sides. As a boy of five it would not be difficult to forget the view from my bedroom window - brickyard chimneys as far as the eye could see and all belching forth great clouds of sulphurous smoke across buildings and countryside alike. Strange as it may seem today, thank goodness, we are far more conscious of pollution and it's harmful affects; forty years ago this was not the case and these pollutants and irritants were taken for granted and accepted as part of the hazard of living near industry. There was no doubting the Italian's ability and desire to work hard in dreadful conditions and in so doing put many of our own countrymen to shame. Saving hard over long years many ventured and invested in new businesses ranging from the building trade through to delicatessens and the rag trade and became a great success whilst naturally merging into the local communities. Not unlike the Chinese and their Chinatown 'quarters' in many cities the Italians created similar 'havens' but never quite so distinct in character, perhaps on account of their European background. Links with the 'old country' are still strong and many of them still ensure they have ample supplies of top quality Italian grapes delivered for wine making purposes - it's something they just couldn't leave behind!

Downing the last mouthfuls of coffee whilst Emilio carefully put the finishing touches to my hair I knew this meant only one thing - I had to step out and take my place in that madhouse and cauldron of the city streets. It wasn't a pleasant thought! But the pressure doesn't end there for I am swept along in a tide of frantic vehicles all seemingly determined to reach their destination just a minute ahead of me or their nearest rival - it has almost become a race to avoid being the chicken! Swept from the city streets along the ring road and onto the A1 I am squeezed, cajoled and jostled in and out of lanes, ticked off and flashed at by the headlights of maniacal drivers seemingly intent on killing themselves and everyone else as we career southwards. It is almost as if I have lost control over the car and where I am travelling - the pressure and weight of traffic is so great! To my horror I suddenly realise that the road I am travelling is no longer as I knew it some 4 or 5 weeks earlier. Where has that delightful thatched cottage gone along with the fine Georgian hotel, and what on earth has happened to those Happy Eater restaurants that once adorned the highway with giant plastic dinosaurs in the children's play areas? Even the old scrap yard with it's heaps of rusting hulks piled high to the sky like some monstrous art creation has been swept away. And where are the old trees and superb hedgerows that delighted us with masses of may blossom whilst we struggled to come to terms with the never ending queues of traffic? It is as if 15 miles of the country has been laid waste in a trice with hardly anything left that is recognizable. As far as the eye can see it is total destruction, with the first worrying signs of what is to come to further wreck our lives and already distraught minds - of course - an 8 lane motorway!

I just cannot contemplate what lies ahead. Thank God I am just 5 hours drive away from the tranquillity of our West Wales village! Life in the slow lane is so pleasant and stress free.

What doesn't get done today might be done in 6 months!

A WALK ON THE WILD SIDE

No one appreciates and understands our 'living countryside' and how, as guardians of a precious heritage, we should care for it for future generations. I would willingly give up my last £1 if someone could prove me wrong! Despite its apparent stubborn resistance to whatever we impose upon it the balance in the countryside is delicate and fragile. Perhaps we all like a challenge in life - if so, this is certainly one of them.

Everyone dreams of a pleasant peaceful walk in the country at the weekend or on a Bank Holiday and that is exactly what some 2 out of every 5 do in Britain. But think long and hard before you venture forth for your Sunday constitutional. Your feet and many thousands more are wearing away recognised footpaths and rights of way often at locations where people know they can walk easily without fear of losing their way or being confronted by barbed wire. There are many more miles of lesser known footpaths, uncared for and almost overgrown beyond use, along which with care we can enjoy the wildlife and scenery.

Just one of those lesser used tracks, near our farmhouse in West Wales - almost totally impassable in places even in the driest of weather - offers the walker a wonderful insight into river valley and mountain scenery at it's most glorious. Although waymarked by the local authority there never appears to be many 'punters'. Perhaps this is a bonus for those living in deeply rural areas where tourism, although important to the local economy, just 'touches' the countryside in such idyllic situations. A cascading mountain river alive with some of the most sought after salmon in Wales, towering valley sides covered with ancient oak woodland and carpeted with indigo rich bluebells and even a marshy area thick with rushes and abounding with woodland plants, birds and butterflies are sights well worth the muddied and sodden shoes. To complete the ethereal and magical scene, set in a clearing towards a turn in the river and upon one of the few level areas, there stands the sad and decaying form of a once active farmhouse and it's outbuildings. It's evocative Welsh name, Clyn Llydan, translates to 'broad valley'. Rural depopulation in this particular valley is rife and as in much of rural Wales it is hardly surprising - farming, unlike the 'bread basket' and 'wheat baron' country of the South East of England, can only be described as marginal in these highly disadvantaged areas. With the farmhouse as it slowly 'returns from whence it came' will go the memories and a culture all of it's own. In it's final throws it still shouts defiance and stubborn resistance to the skies almost as if in some vain and final request for a sympathetic passer by to breath new life into it's weary and worn stones.

As with all 'wild walks' there has to be a bonus for the exertions, preferably at the half way mark, or even earlier if my family had it's way! Choice of beverage and food is even better and marks the little used walk out as one to be endured again - for all the right reasons, of course!

Doorstep sandwiches and a beer or a cream tea with lashings of strawberry jam and cream and a refreshing pot of tea - what a choice! But it's best not to linger or consume too much in case the remaining leg of the walk should turn out to be something of an energy sapping hill climb. My motto has always been 'what goes up must come down' - though there often seems far more 'going up' than 'coming down'! To haul weary bones and full stomachs to the very top of the valley side, acknowledging and recognising various breeds of sheep on the way - a favourite pastime of our family which I suspect is used for ulterior motives in times of supposed hardship - whilst attempting to keep in touch with errant waymarkings, can be crowned with stupendous views across uninterrupted moor and mountain. It's almost as if you are on the very 'top of the world'. The peace, like the views, is stunning. Passing a long abandoned hafod set gloriously at the head of a steep valley we follow a track winding steeply down the valley side alongside it's own babbling mountain stream and retrace the steps of generations of sheep farmers who once used to bring their flocks to summer pasture at the hafod or shieling. This practice is now all but wiped out and the hafod or summer dwelling is no longer a requirement for the Welsh farmer. It is still practised in some parts of Snowdonia but without any further need for residing with the flock in the nearby hafod; the car and the ever advancing layers of tarmac have seen off this most ancient of traditions - transhumance - practised since time immemorial and built around a strict farming calendar. Village and community life revolved around the church, the land

and the seasons. It can be little surprise that farmers rigidly kept to time honoured country habits and 'lore', driving their stock to summer pasture after Spring ploughing and returning them to the hendref, the winter dwelling, on All Saints Day whilst suffering immeasurably harsh and cruel conditions in pitifully poor buildings in the process.

Passing through a working farmyard of a once ancient farmstead I am racked by the many intricate parts that make up this complex jigsaw that is the countryside. Temporarily distracted I divert my gaze to a fine group of vernacular farm buildings set just above the river bank and which appear, more by luck than judgement, to have survived relatively unscathed. Sadly it is no longer a working farm. The presence of teenagers hauling canoes from the river into the yard - which once saw intense farming activity - and parents, plainly packing an already well laden Volvo estate with holiday belongings, imparted a clear message. This was used as a holiday or weekend cottage. But I hear the landowner, village shopkeeper and pub landlord say - 'We need these tourists and their money or how else will our countryside communities survive'.

The tourist and the weekend cottage owner re-echo the 'locals' views -

'Why shouldn't we spend our holiday in the country when we put up with the noise and pollution in town and city - we do at least expect somewhere to buy our groceries and drink a pint when we want'.

In years gone by Wales, rightly or wrongly, has been possessed of an image of rejection of incomers whether they bought property outright or flitted in and out at selected weekends to escape urban life. Tourism in it's broadest sense has been accepted, if somewhat reluctantly, by the indigenous Welsh community - it has even come to be seen as something of a saviour to rural deprivation and reducing farm incomes particularly in the remotest areas where, ironically, the most sensitive landscapes exist.

Each have their point to make but does anyone really listen to the often conflicting views aired by all sides - and what about the toad, badger and the hedgerow birds? Tracks and lanes are a special treasure and haven of flora and fauna peculiar to a valley, hillside or water meadow - in fact you could almost say they were vernacular - they have their own special local 'footprint'. Amidst all the conflicting interests they are the common link.

We certainly don't appreciate the beauty and diversity of the 'vernacular' countryside in our neighbourhood until it is gone or spoilt beyond recognition. Just one careless act or decision by a Council or an individual, whether local or a tourist, can destroy for ever what has taken thousands of years to evolve. To leave a footpath or track to be eventually overtaken by nature may encourage flora and fauna to abound but yet it's limited use could well help to diversify and support the local economy and protect the 'living countryside'. It is a risk that has to be accepted and met head on. We have the power both to destroy but also to conserve whilst the wildlife and woodlands have no right of reply - they just live or die!

We must improve whilst conserving to ensure a 'living' rather than a 'dying' countryside. The dilemma is awesome ....but I'll take the risk and immerse myself with thoughts of those scrumptious cream teas!

BREAKFAST WITH TULIP

'Where's my breakfast?' bleated Tulip.

Tulip is the family favourite - a very large, stubborn yet lovable 13 year old crossbred ewe. Crossbred with what we have never really been sure but for the avid sheep breeders and knowledgeable owners most of her is Speckle Face with possibly a touch of Texel!

When we arrived in West Wales at our 300 year old farmhouse we took responsibility for 8 acres of hillside valley pasture which, with it's own 1 acre broadleaved wood, could only be described as run down and overgrazed. Even from our limited knowledge of pasture and woodland management it was plainly in poor shape. Sadly the pond was overgrown, silted up and being overtaken by invading rushes giving our newly adopted frogs and toads a very hard time. With little time to find suitable 'lawnmowers' to rescue us from the swathes of madly growing grass and having no preconceived ideas about owning stock, sheep or cattle, in desperation we sought help from a neighbour and agreed that his young cattle could 'tack' the land. This proved to be the biggest mistake we had made in our 'new life' in Wales - and we'd only been in residence 3 months! Everything went wrong that could go wrong - but we were new to smallholding and were truly 'green'. The cattle didn't take kindly to the hillside pasture and to crown an awful introduction to farming they succumbed to sunburn! Cows obviously were not the answer.

With a little advice from a helpful local farmer we decided to 'dip our toes in the water' and acquire 4 pedigree Jacob sheep. Mr Griffiths from whom we purchased our new 'family' had been into Jacobs all his farming life regularly showing and winning prizes at the Royal Welsh Show. How he must have laughed at us novices - I'm not sure that at the point of purchase we really knew what we were buying save that each had 4 legs, a head and a tail! The elation on releasing, what we now have to admit, were magnificent sheep into our fields after their bumpy journey from mid Wales was something special - something we shall never forget. Four ewes with a little help from a ram tend to produce offspring and with Jacobs, renowned to be prolific in their prime, what started as a dabble soon burgeoned into a full - blown sheep breeding enterprise. We certainly learnt the hard way.

Orphan lambs are accepted hazards of sheep farming and certainly time consuming - something a farmer with 1000 ewes can ill afford to become immersed in. Quite frequently the task falls to the farmer's wife who, of course, has all the time in the world. Maybe she has a natural instinct and skill with newly born lambs that need constant care and attention - more likely she draws the short straw and is literally left holding the baby!

Tulip arrived one cold February day in the foot well of a battered old Land Rover - she was pathetically small and vulnerable yet with her plaintive bleat so lovable. The loss of her mother immediately after she had just made her entry into the world must have been a shock to such a tiny creature but with bucketfuls of 'TLC' it's amazing how quickly they adapt and place you on a pedestal - mum and provider of food. At this tender age their appetite seems endless as the members of the family noticed as they visited her pen in the barn every 4 hours. She was so small that we often thought we had lost her only to discover her tucked up in a warm nest of straw. Within 3 days, to our great pleasure, but not to our sleep pattern, she had a mate - Taffy - who arrived in similar fashion from the same farmer. He dwarfed Tulip both in size and appetite -a typical ram lamb! Over a period of a year the family poured out affection on Tulip and fought twice to keep her going through life threatening illnesses. Most, if not all farmers, would have considered us totally mad but Tulip repaid us handsomely with many sets of wonderful lambs as well as becoming the darling of the family and a true pet.

Since Tulip and Taffy were brought to us some 12 years ago we have raised many other orphan lambs with great success. Shakespeare, Sage and Snowdrop all came to us in the same way although only Sage and Snowdrop stayed on as breeding ewes, Shakespeare being returned to his original owner, suitably fattened and freezer bound! Even his illustrious name could not save his bacon. For better or for worse it's better born a ewe than a ram - few rams are chosen for the golden accolade with the girls!

This year Tulip became a proud mum yet again with twin lambs, christened Jeremy and Jemima by our two sons. She confidently struts about the meadow making sure that no one takes her favoured position at the head of the melee anxiously waiting for a 'chocolate drop' - sheep nuts to the uninitiated!

'Of course I'm not jealous' she pleads, seeking sympathy. 'I'm just keeping those other funny looking sheep in order. Let's face it apart from the 'boss' Mincepie, one horned Custard and that 'hoover' Maevanwy I'm streets ahead of the rest'. I'm sure she means she is of superior breeding and stock!

'After all this petting and tickling of my leg (which I must admit I really enjoy) ' she muttered 'you still haven't got round to the purpose of your visit - breakfast'.

'Just remember I've got two hungry lambs to feed as well!'

Footnote: At the time of publishing Tulip is now almost 15 years old – and just as loveable!

GATES AND AXEMEN

During our first few years in West Wales we opened up our old farmhouse as a small guesthouse which brought us into contact with people from across Britain and in fact every corner of the globe. It was a fascinating and enlightening time for us both. We were often told in graphic and gory detail the life, times and happenings of every guest's family along with the mayhem and problems they faced in the suburbia we had left for good.

Our guests would often venture into the car park where they had left their latest pride and joy - an up market 16 valve fuel injected 'hotel on wheels' - to double check it was still there, had all it's finery, trim and wheels and ensure it was triple locked, alarmed and fitted correctly with the faithful 'crooklock'! It became a standing joke that we never locked our car or even the barn with its full compliment of expensive agricultural and garden machinery. We could go to bed and sleep easy in the knowledge that it would all be there in the morning but it was quite noticeable that many guests, particularly husbands, were almost paranoid about the security of their treasured vehicle. Their wives, on the other hand, panicked about the safety of their belongings and clothes whilst they were out enjoying the Welsh countryside!

Few, including our insurance company, believe that we reside not only in a gloriously beautiful part of Wales but also the area with the lowest crime rate in the kingdom - apart that is from the Isles of Scilly and some remote Scottish island only inhabited by sea birds and a few sheep! Crime in our locality is a rarity and when it occurs it becomes the centre of heated debate and gossip throughout the village and the outlying areas. Such an event happened not long after we had moved in but it was some days later that we heard through the local 'grapevine' of the mad axe man who had been loose in the area and been subject of an intensive ground and helicopter search. After all the overstatement and hype had been peeled away it turned out to be none other than a local man who, in the words of our neighbourhood policeman, had ' gone off his trolley' whilst in the possession of a small knife! Good enough reason I suppose to apprehend the person in question before he could inflict damage on himself let alone anyone else.

Local criminals took a breather then until some 4 or 5 years later a crime wave hit the neighbourhood - disappearing gates! We first heard of it a month or so after it had begun when it warranted headline news on the front page of our weekly newspaper. Not only had the dastardly villains taken the gates but also the posts that supported them - and at the dead of night! It seemed that there had been an organised gang of gate thieves going around the countryside seeking out easily removable gates. After a few weeks the furore died down and we heard no more. Presumably these 'swines' had either turned their attention to something else or had been caught in the act by a posse of policemen who had set some ingenious trap. As always there was a far more serious side to this almost laughable theft - no gates meant free roaming cows and sheep. But of course the perpetrators of the crimes would never think of that!

There is always a down side to living in an area of rural tranquillity and apparent honest citizens - one day it could change for the worse. Travelling through and parking in large cities where crime of every conceivable kind is rife is something of a shock to us country folk. We are far more vulnerable or as many would say we're just not 'streetwise'.

That reminds me - I'll just go and padlock the barn, lock the car and perhaps I should bring that valuable garden machinery into the house - just in case! I must also remember to prepare the flummery for tomorrow morning's breakfast.

THE LIVING PAST

A colleague who writes nature articles for the local Welsh Life magazine alongside my forays into traditional Welsh buildings recently invited me for afternoon tea at his small cottage with a view to seeking my opinion on his apparently rather fine double seater privy. Knowing that I had been asked by the editor of the Life magazine to pen an article on privies and ty bachs my friend considered it was vitally important for me to see and try out this wonderful creation 'in the flesh'.

Before I could even plan my visit he began to eulogise and expound upon the flora and fauna which was literally on my doorstep - in the field, wood, orchard and even our local churchyard. Conversation was, to say the least, diverse - from lizards to lichens, cowslips to cuckoos, badgers to barn owls, mosses to muntjac and stinking irises to - nothing on earth! It became quite clear that my friend not only had a keen and knowledgeable interest in ornithology and flora but also had an intimate understanding of our village churchyard. He enthusiastically encouraged me to visit and undertake an intensive hands and knees search for a rarity - an orange cowslip!

'How often do they cut the grass?' he asked, sounding almost despairing.

'It's vitally important if this plant is to survive that they mow at the proper time'.

As luck would have it our eldest son had shown a deep interest in unearthing details of past occupants of our ancient farmhouse and frequently made visits to the churchyard to research each and every headstone - much to the amusement of many of his school friends. Several painstaking inspections around the lichen and moss covered gravestones revealed absolutely nothing - that is of the orange cowslip - and so, until the following spring, I could only assume the grass had been cut at the wrong time and these rarities may well have succumbed to an all too keen gardener!

We so often take churchyards for granted. True, they may be the last resting place for a friend, acquaintance or relation but they do represent a wonderful haven for abundant wildlife and flora - untouched, if the grass cutting schedule is rigorously maintained. A leisurely walk makes it abundantly obvious that the modern, smooth polished marble used today by monumental masons gives no assistance whatsoever to the myriad of mosses and lichens which frequently thrive in such unhindered conditions. As my friend so aptly put it

'They've nothing to hold onto'.

Quite true - and we are the losers. In days gone by local sandstone and Welsh slate - the vernacular materials - were always used and gave lichens and mosses a place to cling to and grow without interruption. It also created a local craft industry that almost, without exception, has now vanished just like the village cobbler, carpenter and blacksmith, and dare I say it - the undertaker.

Today's churchyards, if still in use, reflect only too well the spread of 'foreign'; materials to the detriment of the vernacular dialect in an age when local materials, skills and knowledge apparently mean very little. But still these gritty little plants retain their tenacious hold on the older gravestones and with luck on the stonework of the church - as long as the Parochial Church Council hasn't let loose the local builder. Often totally out of touch with historic churches and their micro environment they frequently wreak havoc on the ancient lime mortars, peeling limewash and their 'friends' - the lichens and mosses - by sweeping it all away in favour of a clinical and lifeless alternative where no creatures or plants could hope to survive. The perpetrator is no less than Portland Cement! Few of us appreciate that the presence of these tiny plants is a barometer of our country's and in fact the world's health. A recent television programme highlighted this very fact by spending a considerable amount of time inspecting a churchyard in the wonderful county of Pembrokeshire. The expert declared that there were over 40 different species of lichens and mosses in the churchyard, mostly on the ancient gravestones, and gave the micro community the very highest marks for the quality of it's air. Confirmation, if it were needed, that it was a most healthy place to reside in! As I am not an expert I could not presume to prognosticate upon the air quality around our farmhouse and it's land but from the coverings of lichens on our old oak trees we cannot be far behind the churchyard in Pembrokeshire!

We have made a deliberate policy on our very small farm of leaving selected areas as long grass only cutting when absolutely necessary once all the grasses and wildflowers have had a chance to set seed. The transformation over some years has been truly remarkable with snakes, lizards and all manner of small rodents abounding and providing a wonderful feeding ground for buzzards and red kites and other eager animals attempting to keep nature in balance. Although much of our pasture land has been described as herb rich by the local Farm Stewardship Scheme Officer it could never attain the exalted status of a traditional hay meadow, a feature of the countryside which is now on the 'endangered species list'. The excessively steep valley side of our land alone would preclude any machinery working safely to cut the gently waving grasses and flowers to promote the beginnings of the ultimate goal. Just as the grass in the churchyard and hay meadow have to be coaxed and gently tended over many years so many are persuaded and encouraged by colourful and convincing advertising that they can successfully 'sow' a hay meadow from a packet of wildflower seeds which will give them delight and pleasure for years to come. Disillusionment only too often sets in as the delight is frequently short lived or doesn't arrive at all despite all the wonderful promises on the packaging. They have been cruelly misled!

As one old Cotswold farmer once told me

'You can't make a hay meadow - you'm have to create it, boy!'

And as he so rightly pointed out it can take up to 20 years or more. Creation doesn't work fast! The few hay meadows that do survive are quite literally hundreds of years old and are the end product of caring country folk who had the skill, knowledge and will to maintain them as an essential part of the farm and good husbandry. There is no doubt it is a skill lost but to a few.

Despite the paucity of hay meadows, in May the meadow grasses and accompanying wildflowers across our fields bow gracefully in the gentle breezes whilst the air is full and heavy with myriad fragrances. Ewes and their lambs bask in the warmth, reclining amongst the bright new greensward whilst Marmaduke, the old farm cat, sets out once more, almost unseen amidst the tall grass, to the furthest outpost of his territory. Marmaduke no longer resides on the farm but two doors away since the previous occupants of our property discovered he did not take kindly to being uprooted and moved to Worcestershire and continually tried to return to his old haunts some 150 miles distant. Now almost next door to his 'old home' he still 'rules OK' and defiantly considers our farm is still his against all comers. He regularly passes the backdoor of the farm with a treasured prize of a vole or a mouse which more often than not has come from our orchard or even our Top Meadow some half a mile away!

Marmaduke has a colleague, or maybe he is the sworn enemy - the churchyard cat, Mog - a fluffed up black and white creature that appears to have been subjected to regular visits to the tumble dryer! Certainly out of the same mould, Mog is tenacious, fearsome and master of all he surveys as he perches on one of the ancient gravestones - no doubt he has rich pickings amongst the cowslips, mosses and lichens.

He is but just another player in the living churchyard. Those voles and mice should watch out!

Footnote: The old stone walls and lime mortar of our farmhouse host Rusty Back Ferns (Asplenium ceterach) - a splendid addition that gives the old building a truly well worn rural feel.

It is sad to report that Marmaduke is no more and Mog also seems to have disappeared – their replacements are not a patch on them!

AS TIME GOES BY
(OR ODE TO A SHEEP)

It's mid February and sitting in my cosy office I contemplate what has been and what is to come. I look across our land that climbs steeply up the valley side, away to our one acre wood where I can see red kites wheeling effortlessly silhouetted against a crimson sunset. The ash and oak shorn of their leafy cover some months ago stand like giant skeletons against the falling light. The weather has been cold and inhospitable until now but today the first harbingers of spring have appeared as they always do. The snowdrops are bowing their heads in the orchard and the big Jacob ewes, heavy in lamb, and close at hand in Home Meadow, are feeding contentedly at the hayrack knowing their time has almost come. Within the next week or so there will be new life with lambs gambolling across the meadow - spring is just round the corner.

But yet life is so unfair, for the older you become the faster time flies - it seems like only yesterday that it was lambing time last year. The shepherd's calendar is followed ritualistically in Wales and takes precedence over many events which to many would seem far more important and relevant. To all but the fully accredited and initiated flock owner it must seem a fuss over nothing. But when there are three times as many sheep in Wales as human population it is not difficult to see why life, particularly in the rural areas, revolves around these woolly creatures. Indeed not to talk about sheep can make you feel isolated! Not until we had owned our own small flock for a few years did we come to realise how easily and effortlessly you click into 'automatic pilot' for the four main events of the calendar - dipping, shearing, tupping and of course lambing. Living in towns and cities before our move to Wales we had no idea or recognition of the hard work needed to keep sheep healthy and fit. To us, like many others, they were just woolly animals on the hillside with four legs, a head and a tail!

The annual round of dipping has for the first time in the living memory of many flock owners and shepherds been called into question, and quite rightly so. The dip may have little effect upon the health of a sheep, in essence a short lived creature, but it's toll on humans handling the deadly chemical has become only too apparent in the worst possible manner. It had to change. As always in such cases the benefits may have helped the farmer and his health but there is a deadly sting in the tail! The newly promoted and used dip can now devastate a watercourse and all it's inhabitants with but just a drop! It is a fair question to ask why we have to dip sheep considering that before these lethal chemicals were ever introduced animals took their chance but quite often succumbed to a nasty lingering death. We are now, no doubt, far more conscious and aware of preventing unnecessary suffering and ensuring animals remain productive for as long as possible - but at a cost.

Shearing has never held the same insurmountable problems although many a farmer rightly complains at the miserable pittance he receives for the fleeces, a natural product of the sheep. Today it barely covers the cost of the shearers who sweat gallons as they swiftly move through the flock leaving sheep looking more like goats and certainly very 'sheepish' as they are parted from their woolly overcoat in such an undignified manner! June is the month for shearing and with our small flock which takes about an hour to attend to it can almost be guaranteed the weather will be either atrociously wet or abominably hot! Mike, our friendly Welsh farmer from just up the valley, endeavours to bring in his weighty shearing machine between the spells of continuous heavy rain. Inevitably he finds himself working in steamy heat surrounded by masses of flies and the remnants of tail end fleeces. As I'm sure happened in generations past shearing, like the harvest, is a family and often community affair which wouldn't be complete without ice cold beer at the completion of labours. Meanwhile willing helpers lay out and roll the fleeces ready for bagging for early collection by the mills. Modern day shearing machines are heavy and difficult to operate but they can be as nothing to when 1000 sheep had to be clipped by hand shears! A true art and labour of love.

Shearing may be a busy and tiring time for the farmer but by the time tupping has arrived he can sit back and watch the action! A new year in the life of the flock has begun and the rams, fresh from their holidays with the 'lads', can start to strike up 'relationships' with up to 80 ladies! It has become something of a pastime with our two sons as they count the red marks on the ewes' backs as tupping progresses into October and November. They remark on those who have fallen prey to the proud ram and the antics of some of the younger ewes vainly attempting to escape. Worn out and looking for a break the ram retires to a distant field, his work done for another year, whilst we start the countdown in the diary to first lambing - 147 days away!

Lambing is a time of hope and new life but also tired and aching limbs that result from many a nerve racked hour watching, waiting and often assisting the ewe to deliver twins or even triplets. For almost a month there is no such thing as a comfortable unbroken 8 hours tucked up in bed under the duvet - waking and sleeping hours merge into one until the last of the ewes has delivered her offspring. Quite frequently the last to lamb out seems to have inside knowledge of our battered and weary constitution and uncharitably drags out the inevitable until she can hold out no more. At last the 2 hours on and 2 hours off shift system comes to an end and we sink into our bed as if it were a pleasure we had not enjoyed for years rather than weeks whilst we mull over the ups and downs of lambing. The downs, when lambs or even mothers are lost, drain us physically and mentally but often it is short lived as we help a set of twins into the world. We reflect upon our work or rather that of the ewe and the ram and the delightful lambs wobbling on unsteady legs around the meadow - in a few days they will be pronking and playing with boundless energy!

Spring is in the air - in 12 months we shall be lambing again!

Tempus fugit.

A RURAL PRACTICE
OR
ON THE WAITING LIST

A large ominous looking brown envelope arrived one morning in our post recently and our thoughts immediately turned to the dreaded Inland Revenue chasing up long forgotten and unknown monies. To our complete surprise the envelope was overprinted with the local Health Authority insignia and staring out from the little 'window' were the words 'The Surgery'.

We had known for some time that our ancient farmhouse in generations past had been the scene of many a family christening and wedding with these happy events providing a good excuse for the whole village community to join in and 'let their hair down'. There is no doubt that these community gatherings were not that uncommon as was the elevated status given to the Head Teacher of the village school, the Vicar and the local Doctor. In those days of glorious summers, harsh winters, appalling working conditions and rife poverty it is hardly surprising in such a 'simple' life, where each relied on everyone else, that these 'icons' of the community were revered and placed on a pedestal! It was not that far removed from medieval society when the priest and the lord of the manor held sway and were regarded as pillars of society apparently unable to do any wrong!

How things have changed in the past generation - and some would say for the worst. It had been accepted in village life for the doctor to hold surgery in the biggest and most capacious farmhouse, that most akin to the Manor House or Manor Farm. In our village our spacious kitchen was the venue for surgeries until he relocated temporarily to one of the pubs before an up market surgery and health centre was established some 8 miles distant from the village. There can be surely little wrong with this now redundant 'hands on' approach in bringing medical care to rural communities. In the countryside, where the car had not taken a stranglehold on society, it was expected that health care should be delivered to your doorstep. I can remember my father recalling how the travelling 'medicine man' called in their fen village selling all manner of potions and ointments to his parents - and that was only some 50 years ago! However the use of the local pub as a base for dispensing cures and offering judgement on various ailments conjures up vivid imaginations of the GP having a 'quick half' before departing for the next village! Maybe this 'community care' was not such a bad way of bringing relief and support to the countryside after all - it is certainly a lot different to the situation that doctors and hospitals face today.

There is little doubt that today we have lost the 'individual' touch and contact which meant so much. It is hardly surprising considering the demands now placed on a Health Service stretched to breaking point, a victim of it's own success, the massive advances in medical knowledge and treatment and the increasing longevity of the nation's population. It is a well known fact that some patients now wait so long for treatment that by the law of averages they eventually finish up becoming emergencies and costing far more to the public purse. Initial consultation and preventative treatment may well have ensured they did not become a 'statistic' in an already overcrowded hospital.

The patient's situation could be easily likened to an historic building neglected and refused grant assistance on the grounds that it is of insufficient architectural merit and age. Holier than thou bureaucrats who have no concept of the importance of local and traditional heritage ensure another landmark becomes another 'statistic' of the heritage, abandoned and left to 'return from whence it came' all those years ago. Sadly old buildings in the principality do not count despite their wonderful contribution to an often stunning landscape. Unless some kind, beneficent fairy godmother with a heart literally of gold is spirited out of the nation the local heritage will lose yet another vital 'limb'. How long can we stand by and watch? How long can we staunch the haemorrhaging?

Our doctors now have a brand new Health Centre kitted out with the latest technology and equipment but still the system cannot cope. Authoritative and august bodies now claim that hitherto 'defeated' diseases such as polio, diphtheria and tuberculosis, once the scourge of our population, will return with a vengeance to haunt us once more. Many experts rightly point to our over zealous use of antibiotics - the wonder drug - which is about to cause our downfall if only we did but take notice. It is almost a certainty that the population at large would never allow this proven means of controlling and defeating all comers to be limited or removed from the shelves. At some point we have to make a momentous decision - not just for us in this tiny island but across the whole globe.

The waiting is almost over - time is running out for our health and heritage!

VIII

TROUBLED
TRANQUILITY

A BRIDGE TOO FAR

A local retired farmer and villager stood chewing the cud on the ancient bridge over the river occasionally glancing at the stupendous view and nodding sagely about some no doubt extremely important issues.

The peace and quiet of the riverside setting was shattered, if only momentarily, by the sudden appearance of an enormous tractor on gargantuan wheels towing a trailer in its wake. The correspondents on the bridge seemed totally unperturbed, almost as if they had expected the vehicle to turn round (if it could) and return up the mountain road from which it had come or, spend the rest of the morning manoeuvring into position to pass over the bridge. After some reversing and muttering of oaths by the driver our correspondents were eventually forced to retreat in the face of the oncoming machinery. Once the tractor had inched it's way across the bridge and roared off down the village street our friends lazily returned to the same spot on the bridge to resume their conversation and gaze into the distance. Everything returned to its normal peaceful existence and village and wildlife quietly went about its duties. Our two correspondents must have run out of conversation for very shortly they retraced their steps across the bridge and went their separate ways down the sleepy village street. It was siesta time.

If the Highways Department and our local Councillor had their way this would all change and the bridge and it's valley setting would be destroyed forever. Not content with obliterating ancient bridges in the name of European directives they seem happy, nay gratified, that they can eliminate structures deemed not to 'fit the standards'.

Over breakfast one morning whilst scanning the local newspaper I noticed tucked away in one corner a Planning Application which alarmingly heralded the almost total destruction and rebuilding of a fine Listed bridge which spans one of our local rivers within a spectacular setting. How could they contemplate it and for what good reason? They say it was to improve the local economy! It would be their intention to double the width of this fabulous bridge so that large lorries could reach a handful of scattered farms by a precipitous narrow mountain road complete with hairpin bends! It seemed to have escaped the attention of the councillor that these farms could be more easily reached from a totally different direction without recourse to circumnavigating the offending bridge. The Highways Department raised an ugly spectre in cahoots with the councillor and no doubt the farmers 'affected' by the awkward bridge and would move heaven and earth to secure their deadly intentions. I am convinced in this part of Wales there are night 'hit squads' seeking out poor defenceless ancient bridges which they would plot to destroy and replace with modern sanitised safety conscious concrete carbuncles! As with everything involving Highways there are always two overriding reasons for throwing away our heritage with not as much as a thought - road safety and inability to meet the current 'standards'. So what!

'But the bridge must be replaced so that the new 'heavyweight' lorries can pass safely'.

What about banning these ever expanding lorries and allowing only small trucks to deliver goods to rural areas?

'Out of the question' came the indignant reply.

'The present bridge does not meet the standards and must be replaced'.

The great Road God in the sky has spoken!

I fervently believed some years ago when living in Cambridgeshire that the attitude in the rural bliss of Wales must surely be different to the 'car led' society I had experienced in what was rapidly becoming one vast urban sprawl connected by the ever advancing tentacles of dual carriageways and motorways. How wrong I was! Apparently glorious countryside complimented by the all too scarce country lanes and bridges does not produce a different breed of Engineer or Highways Officer. If anything these philistines along with County and Community Councillors and, in may cases, residents, seem hell bent on performing environmental suicide. They seem intent on turning a rural idyll into what I thought I had left behind for good in England - a concrete and 'blacktop' jungle where the car and juggernaut rule supreme! I once thought that this wanton destruction in the name of jobs and progress and the avowed aim to cut 5 minutes from journey times was the domain of the unscrupulous developer and Government Departments. Wrong again!

Early one morning I received a telephone call from a Welsh lady who had read one of my articles in the local press. It highlighted the urgent need to protect and conserve what was left of our built heritage (including bridges) for our children and their children to come, for their fulfilment and enjoyment. I was soundly ticked off! How dare I even consider this and force people to live in outdated, draughty houses just because I said they were old and important. She insisted that all old buildings should be demolished as already more than enough had been re-erected and were on display for all to see at the Welsh Folk Museum in St. Fagans.

'What do we want with these decrepit buildings?' she ranted.

I was tempted to ask her if she would rather see the whole of Wales 'concreted over' but I resisted the temptation and politely accepted her points and the conversation came to a close. I gracefully agreed to disagree with her! I still cannot comprehend how anyone, even the most insensitive of us, could contemplate losing some of the most stunning countryside and the heritage which compliments it. The bridge that is under threat lies in a landscape of breathtaking quality with glorious forest backdrops of ancient oak woodland and later coniferous plantations that 'glow' deep red and orange in the autumn.

Perhaps it is time for village and rural communities to wake up to the stark reality of the losses in the countryside and stand shoulder to shoulder over the sacrilege some public servants, the 'great and the good' and a misguided few wish to perpetrate in the name of progress.

This time they have gone too far!

Footnote: The delightful bridge and it's superb setting are safe - we won the day and the 'destroyers' left with their tails between their legs! But for how long?

LOSING OUR WAY

The village we moved to in West Wales after our sojourn in the bleak landscape of Eastern England was the extreme opposite in every respect. Friends and relations were sure that we would be cast off far from civilisation as they conjured up vivid descriptions of the family marooned for weeks or even months halfway up a mountainside. They were convinced we had made the wrong decision - Wales was for sheep and not for people!

Some of the villagers seeing us as incoming, soft and unwary English played on the well known and legendary weather - rain and wind and plenty of it. One of our neighbours, who happens to live some 500 feet above us at the top of the valley threw down the gauntlet one chilly winter morning outside the village school. Having deposited her 'charges' at the school gate and finished her duties as a school taxi to the outlying farmsteads she pinned me to the wall with her intensely descriptive details of what I could expect from the weather. I was left in no doubt that we had made the wrong choice - we would experience weather far worse than either my family or I had ever endured! Tales of woe focused around weeks when temperatures never lifted above minus 10 centigrade, snow lay level with the hedge tops in the lanes and the community would be cut off from civilisation for weeks on end! She was no doubt well meaning in her endeavours but little realised that I had just returned from the East the day before having suffered 4 or more days of freezing fog, 50 yard visibility, disastrously high pollution levels and with temperatures not lifting above minus 15 at night. I had been frozen to the marrow and longed for the comparative mild comfort of Wales. The village was truly like a Turkish bath to me - it basked in just minus 1centigrade! She was right about thing though - electricity failures. We have discovered they are quite common place but not, as our neighbour suggested, the result of foul weather but rather the wayward habits of local farmers and their errant machinery. We still suffer horizontal rain but our once moist, warm coastal influenced climate is rapidly being replaced by drier and Saharan like summers; the winters just seem to get wetter, if that is possible!

Our friend with the school taxi was only trying to be helpful in the broadest sense like everyone else in the village but we must have appeared like visitors from another planet to such an insular and rural community. To our utter astonishment and amazement we discovered that many of the village inhabitants had been no further than the local 'mart' in their lifetime of some 60 or 70 years - often only a once or twice weekly event to sell or buy stock and have a good chinwag with a few farmer friends. Of course the annual Royal Welsh Show at Builth Wells provided for some the highlight of the year, almost as good as an annual holiday, where they could enjoy and soak up the very best in Welsh farming enterprise. Thank goodness the show has retained its true family and rural atmosphere - much against the national trend.

One of our neighbours who lived in the Council houses across the lane from our farmhouse had been born and bred in the village and never felt the need to travel further than the local market town on Wednesdays and Saturdays. Not long after moving in we heard the tragic news that she had passed away but thankfully both our two boys and ourselves had already had the pleasure of sitting entranced in her living room as she recalled life in the village. According to her the lane alongside our land that fed many vehicles into the village was just a muddy farm track when she was a child! Her talk of farming and village life during her childhood and teenage days was fascinating and intriguing, particularly her vivid description of the antics of the young lads and lassies in the hay loft above the byre of our very own farmhouse. Enjoying a refreshing cup of tea and a generous slice of homemade fruit cake we sat enthralled as she recounted with great delight her younger days and her obvious real concern over the loss of a very ancient right of way - one which her parents and grandparents before, and no doubt untold generations of local people, had used almost every day of their lives. She recalled with impressive clarity people on horseback regularly using the 'sunken green lane' as a route between the village and outlying communities such as Brechfa and Gwernogle. It seemed that it had been used by many for attending the Parish Church or Chapels long before the internal combustion engine even came on the scene. Even after the car had arrived such 'green lanes' still served a vitally important role for the farmer and of course the walker and horse riders out to enjoy the countryside to the full. Our neighbour reflected with great sadness that both planners and villagers had not opposed a request for a bungalow to be built over the 'green lane' effectively stopping it up for good. She would be mortified at the present prospect of yet another property and it's garden being superimposed across the lane, or what remains of it - even the upper reaches have now been barred by stock fencing and barbed wire ironically a direct result of a farm stewardship scheme backed by the Welsh Office! Our immediate neighbour, lately from the affluent South East, and appearing to have no love of rights of way, recently found to his cost the penalty of having a property and garden straddling a 'green lane'. Two horse riders, following the remnants of the right of way, arrived in his beloved urban style garden seeking passage and exit into the village lane! The shock must have been almost too much for him but he had little option but to let them through. If he had not known before that his property lay over an unextinguished right of way he certainly knew after horse and riders had traversed his garden!

Local authorities have a legal obligation to all residents to compile a register of public footpaths, bridleways and rights of way and ensure that these rights are maintained for free and unhindered access to everyone. Green lanes or roads, as in our village, appear in the majority of cases to have 'slipped the net' despite their acknowledged age and importance in the countryside. Our 'sunken green lane' interconnects with a network of other trackways and drovers' roads up the side of the hill to a 1000 feet and then down into the Cothi valley dissecting, as it goes, prehistoric field systems and settlements. It is a sad reflection on our outlook to life that even though our ancient 'green lane' has been conveniently missed from registration like so many others it received no sympathy from those wishing to erect one of the all pervasive bungalows - another statistic in the bungalow blitz of Wales. Let's face it the lane was a total inconvenience which meant nothing in the face of building a new 'home'. Do they realise the local history they have destroyed with a single swipe of a JCB? It is far too easy these days to 'steamroller' through our local history, environment and built heritage with complete abandon and impunity - no one seems to care anymore. It obviously means absolutely nothing to many of the population in their determination to 'live' as they wish with not a thought for anyone or anything else!

The incident over our 'green lane' reminded me of the legal battle which blew up recently in an otherwise peaceful well behaved corner of prosperous England over the rights of a hedgerow to remain in the face of determined supporters and members of a bowling club intent on extending their facilities. Club officials saw the tatty hedgerow as but a small inconvenience and nuisance and certainly not something that would completely ruin their plans. Fortune was on the side of the threatened hedgerow in the guise of a highly enlightened, educated and determined person who, having done his homework on the rights and privileges of hedgerows, stood up and defiantly defended this apparent small piece of the countryside. The officials and members of the club were 'bowled out' with no reply in the courts - the nice gentleman, and his hedgerow that dated back to the time of the Enclosure Acts, winning hands down! The decision of the court was final - the hedgerow must stay despite the protestations of the Bowling Club. Sense had prevailed.

It is to be hoped that with the introduction of the recent hedgerows legislation the law will at last support and uphold the retention and enhancement of a national asset along with it's 'freeholders'. Hopefully footpaths and green lanes will benefit and survive alongside their natural neighbours and companions. It would be unimaginable to consider our once green and pleasant land devoid of hedgerows, leafy footpaths and lanes - landmarks in our universally popular pursuit of walking.

We truly will have lost our way!

TRAMS AND TRANSISTORS

A few years ago it may not have been popular to be a supporter of the return of the tram, the resurgence in the use of the bicycle with their own dedicated routes or attempts to discover alternative, cheap and non - polluting fuels for our cars - but times are changing. Many of our large cities have already committed themselves to reinstating the tram and some have even built elevated or street level 'metros'. A good many people look on these authorities as either very brave and forward looking or downright foolish in the face of the iron grip that the internal combustion engine has inflicted on the population.

In the countryside transport could never be viewed in this way, purely on the grounds of economics - and this cannot be disputed. Unfortunately few country dwellers take time out to consider how important transport maybe to them and take the car, the occasional bus to town and the school bus all very much for granted. Our villages could never hope to support any environmentally friendly urban transport system but a blend of old and new technology and a little foresight and self help would go a long way to assisting in the drive for a cleaner and safer environment.

The telephone rang out one afternoon at about quarter to five - our eldest son had yet to put in an appearance on the school bus.

'Is Christopher home yet?' enquired the obviously worried parent. 'Our son should have been home over half and hour ago'.

School buses, a central part of Welsh country life, are vulnerable not just to the whims and fancies of the mandarins at County Hall but more often than not to the vagaries of the weather, mechanical failures and the frailties and idiosyncrasies of the drivers. The 'vintage' of some of the vehicles used defies imagination and certainly the maniacal attitude of some drivers leaves me scared and cold! It is an unwritten policy in our household never to venture out or drive down our narrow village lane to the main road between the hours of 8 and 9 in the morning or 4 and 5 in the afternoon - unless of course you are not that fussed at being forced off the road, crushed between a bus and the roadside hedge or intimidated by a 5 tonner breathing down your exhaust pipe. It is not that uncommon for the school bus to wantonly demolish the parapets of the village bridge or clip the side off a car opposite the Post Office whilst the school children gaze on in rapturous excitement at the frantic and hopeless gesticulations of the driver. You could almost write the accident report. 'Well, you see officer .....er .....this bridge came out and hit my vehicle - honest!'

Christopher eventually arrived home some hour and a half late with hot news - the bus had run out of fuel! Oh for a modicum of technology in this quiet rural backwater. Christopher wittingly pointed out that a notice stuck to the dashboard of the vehicle and glaring straight at the driver read 'Please check fuel levels before leaving the depot'.

I loath and hate mobile phones particularly when I find myself behind a driver using one hand to ensure his conversation is uninterrupted whilst using the other to steer his vehicle down a twisting country lane at 50 mph! How stupid can people be? But I do admit they do have their uses - in the right place! For some unknown reason both County Council and the bus companies they employ for the 'school runs' have failed to acknowledge that a mobile phone in each bus could save a lot of heartache and expense and put parents minds at rest. Some 14 months on since the 'incident' the bus still chugs on regardless without the assistance of modern technology - all for the sake of a couple of hundred pounds!

Maybe in Wales we can't take advantage of the highly advanced transport systems now installed or planned across the kingdom but at least we should recognise that a very small piece of 20th. Century technology could help keep our struggling rural transport system on the straight and narrow. The drivers may be suicidal and unpredictable but at least that minute computer chip and transistor could be a lifeline when all else fails.

Footnote: August 2006. It now seems that the County Council are to install CCTVs in school buses.

BEYOND THE CALL OF DUTY

Sitting in a comfortable armchair one cold winter's evening browsing through the pages of the local weekly newspaper little expecting to uncover anything contentious, my eyes alighted upon the photograph of a rural scene I immediately recognised. Scouring the supporting article it soon became clear that the author, a born and bred Welshman, had an almighty axe to grind about an historic event that quite reasonably had been presumed, by various academics, to have taken place on the very land depicted in the photograph.

The event, a battle between the Welsh and the English, had supposedly taken place in 1257, over 750 years ago, at the height of the 'animosity' when the Welsh did not take kindly to being invaded and 'tamed' by their neighbours. The fields which represent the battle site are today, peaceful, grazed by cattle and sheep and adorned by carpets of buttercups in spring; they do not even hint at what might have taken place all those years ago. As yet, there is no clamour for hard evidence to be unearthed through excavation, all protagonists, for the moment, relying on documented evidence however dubious and unreliable. No one has stepped forward to testify to finding human remains, undeniably the result of battle, or other artefacts of war - swords, spears, shields and helmets. Maybe there are none!

Having mysteriously escaped the notice of the Ordnance Survey the somewhat over zealous, self taught historian had put pen to paper in an almost laughable attempt of accusing the map makers, naturally English, of a cynical ploy to 'rubbish' the Welsh and one of their more dubious victories over the 'old enemy'. The writer seemed quite adamant that the 'English' Ordnance Survey were blatantly trying to annoy their neighbours 'across the dyke' and denigrate a sacred national monument.

This rumbustiousness reminds me of the events that surrounded the alarming announcement that the Ministry of Transport were planning to plough a four lane motorway across the site of the Battle of Naseby. Potentially this involved the lifting and re internment of many human remains known to lie beneath the peaceful meadows. Sadly the Ministry, in their normal ham fisted and blunt approach, did not appear to recognise that those who fell in battle and lay at rest under the Northamptonshire soil were just as sacrosanct as those who lost their lives at sea and went down with their vessels, be it in Tudor times or more recently. Those under the sea have, generally, been left to rest in peace possibly, and cynically, some would say, as governments would find the cost of raising them too much to bear! Unfortunately, it seems it is only too easy for sites on land to be deemed easy meat and far less contentious. The uproar was predictable and quite understandable - opposition was voiced across the nation and around the world!

At least the presumed battlefield of Coed Clathen, in the heart of West Wales, is not, and is never likely to be under threat of being engulfed by a four lane motorway! The irate local historian should be mighty thankful for small mercies! Never one to deliberately and provocatively show up the native Welsh for their all too frequent habit at hitting out at what they see as their arrogant neighbours, I'm afraid to say the deeply offended historian had got it wrong! There is evidence in ancient annals of a battle in the area; on delving through my vast stock of maps I uncovered a tattered 1st. Series Ordnance Survey map printed in 1959 which proudly announced the site of the Battle of Coed Clathen of 1257! It seems the unseen bureaucrats at Ordnance Survey should be exonerated from an ignominious felony although no doubt if I were to announce this I would be branded a traitor to the Welsh cause!

So deep is native resentment that the recent announcement by the Courts that a certain Port Authority, far down west, should pay a fine of some £4m for admitting their responsibility in the fatal Sea Empress disaster and the environmental catastrophe that followed meant the media turned on the Court's judgement; they accused them of putting down the Welsh and an already struggling economy! What seemed to have escaped the ranting media was that a Welsh Port Authority had neglected their duties and failed to protect a fragile environment and economy. The fault lay fair and square in Wales at their very own doorstep!

Introvert, reactionary, small minded, resistant to change and insular - just a few ways to describe a principality in turmoil and at war with itself. Anti authoritarian could quite readily be added to the list considering what happened with the Sea Empress and what is known to go on quite openly within all walks of life in Wales. I am told many a time that it is nothing like this - rather the Welsh are totally misunderstood! One thing is certain - anyone other than native Welsh find many of the indigenous population confusing, arrogant and belligerent and obviously still bearing grudges from centuries past! Many 'immigrants', as they are quite frequently known, do not make it a top priority to return to the principality, once they have left – and it's not surprising! As an Englishman and Fenman and proud of my 'roots' I certainly don't make a habit of reminding the Welsh of where I come from and singing the praises of St. George and Hereward the Wake.

One day, at the local village school, I was approached and accosted by a buxom Welsh lady.

'You'll be shouting for Wales on Saturday, won't you?'

The Five Nations Rugby Tournament was upon us once more when the blood of every Welshman runs passionate and the papers are overtaken by every imaginable detail and angle on the forthcoming game. Red fiery Welsh dragons glare at you from every page!

Support Wales when I'm an Englishman!

Never! That is beyond the call of duty!

Footnote: Apologies to the Italians – they have since joined making it the Six Nations Rugby Tournament.

TROUBLESOME TOILETS

My next door neighbour was propping up the bar in the village shop as was his daily ritual. Otherwise the pub appeared deserted with not even the landlord or his wife in sight.

'Don't see you up here often' was his comment.

'What's dragged you up here?'

'Toilets' I replied.

He looked bemused and mystified. When the landlord appeared from somewhere in the depths of the pub announcing with almost conceited satisfaction 'They're all in there - waiting for you' my neighbour looked decidedly worried and uncomfortable.

The thought of missing a mouthful of thirst quenching beer seemed to drift over him and he returned, as if on automatic pilot, to his pint balanced so carefully on the beer mat. Of course I could read his mind! Why was he the only patron in the bar and where was the rest of the village? As I turned with some apprehension to make my way into the adjoining meeting room my eyes became fixed upon a stuffed pike glaring down at me from inside a glass case suspended above the bar. It didn't look very friendly! What would meet me on the other side of the door? At that moment the vicar crashed through the pub door and broke my immediate train of thought.

'Are you ready Ken? Let's go in'.

He's fine I thought - he's got someone on his side up there rooting for him. I recollected the biblical story of

David in the lion's den as I tamely followed the vicar whilst still wistfully glancing back at that awesome pike!

The village toilets saga has been rumbling on for more years than residents cared to think. At long last after 20 years of cogitating and pondering the Community Council had shown their hand much to the disgust and total opposition of the village. Community life relies on a shop and post office for survival far more than public toilets and having learnt of the imminent demise of this treasured asset villagers had earmarked a small plot of land, held in trust by the Council, as the site for a Community Shop and Post Office. Fate determined that the Community Council also had designs on the land even though it had taken them some 20 years to think of it. There is nothing more certain than such arrogance by an elected body to persuade villagers to arrange a public meeting at which they can harangue and berate their wayward representatives. The meeting room was packed to the rafters with many unknown faces all, no doubt, from the various outlying farms in the parish. There was hardly any standing room save for a few close to the door that led directly into the bar!

The meeting, manfully chaired by the vicar, was at times overheated and Councillors were left in little doubt as to the feelings of their electorate - the toilets were given the thumbs down! As the meeting broke up and people drifted to the bar little did the vicar and I, or in fact anyone else, realise that 12 months on we would be re - treading the very same steps, staring that same stuffed fish in the eye and striving to conjure up ways of taking the heat out of what was guaranteed again to be a lively and inflamed debate.

The Community Council had not learnt their lesson - they still did not acknowledge the vociferous opposition to their proposals and defiantly pressed on to provide a facility that no one wanted, no one would use and something which could become a target of abuse for all the wrong reasons. Urgent telephone calls to the Local Authority and the Ombudsman failed to raise any hopes that we could hold the Community Council liable for ignoring valid opposition and breaching their powers. It confirmed my own worst fears - the Council could act above the law as they were totally unaccountable. As the ombudsman so quaintly put it to me

'Let's face it - their greatest project might well be restricted to erecting a bus stop sign or placing a public seat in the centre of the village. They're small players when all said and done'.

Maybe in many communities but 'developments' in our village were becoming seriously heavy!

'If you don't agree with their decisions dump them at the next election - vote them out!'

Despite a further public meeting under the glare of that fish, an exchange of bitter and acrimonious letters and a staggering show of opposition in a mile long petition the Councillors persisted. They insisted the toilets were vital for visitors and of course the tug of war team who competed on the show field some half a mile distant. A local friend, who happened to be an avid opponent of the terrible toilets, and who is nothing but fair minded, reflected on the Councillors dogged persistence.

'The tug of war team and it's followers are hardly likely to use any public toilets' he exclaimed 'when the village pub is on the doorstep of the show field. The lure of the beer would be far too great! And what visitors? We don't get any!'

He has a point.

Several well meaning people suggested that I should stand for election as a Community Councillor when the current incumbents term of office expired in 2 years time. I was showered with offers of support and encouragement but why were they so keen to see me in the 'hot seat' rather than themselves?

Should you take the plunge and join the merry band of councillors listen and place yourself in the shoes of the electorate and never underestimate the power of the common people.

If you don't want to be sucked into a troublesome toilets saga choose your councillors well - you have been warned!

Footnote: For the avid troublesome toilet saga watcher it is worth pointing out that a further 6 years has elapsed and still the little building is nowhere in sight - not that we mind of course. Long may the village have no public toilets!

We still have our village shop, primary school, church, two chapels and two pubs!

LIKE LAMBS TO THE SLAUGHTER

Last autumn we were bombarded with glossy literature and harangued to return once more to those gloomy and miserable polling booths, usually housed in the local chapel or school, to put a cross against - not this time a candidates name but a simple Yes or No. Having gone through a similar ritual some 4 or 5 months previously this time we were told it would be our one and only opportunity to have freedom over our own affairs and throw off the shackles of the Union and all it has supposedly meant to the oppressed Welsh. Yes - it was Devolution time!

The principality had some years before put itself through similar heart searching and self flagellation yet decided unanimously that it would remain better off under the status quo despite the vociferous cries of the Welsh Language Society and many others with little vision or idea of what might lie ahead under 'self rule'. As an 'outsider' of some 12 years standing or so, who will probably not be 'accepted' for at least another 10 years or more I still fail to see what all the fuss is about. Why put Home Rule ahead of far more pressing issues which affect the man in the street? We are today, when all said and done, not greatly unlike our ancestors who roamed this fair land many thousands of years ago without a shred of our modern living. Most people are just concerned they have a roof over their heads, food in their belly and enough spare cash so that they can have a fling and enjoy themselves occasionally - it little matters to most whether the Secretary of State and the Prime Minister happen to be Geordie or Brummie and neither can speak a word of Welsh. Some who think they speak for the majority and probably like to hear the sound of their own voice try to persuade us we have been under the 'hammer' of the English, the 'old enemy', ever since the Union. They are aided and abetted by the local press who seem to thrive on goading the populace into outbursts of nationalistic outpourings and hurling insults at anyone or anything not Welsh. Maybe these people have a gigantic 'chip' on their shoulder or they are stuck in a rut and can't even lift themselves above the parapet for fear of being sniped at. The defiant 'last stand' mentality has done little to enhance the 'Welshness' of the principality or persuade hesitant 'outsiders' to participate in learning the ancient Celtic language with it's strong mystical, musical and poetic connections. The Reverend Eli Jenkins in Dylan Thomas's 'Under Milkwood' declared -

'Praise the Lord - we are a musical nation'.

A proud and no doubt justified claim but of little value when the Welsh wantonly watch over their 'whole culture' being eroded at an alarming rate. The Welsh language cannot stand on it's own despite the bilingual policies and financial investment of Government and public bodies alike and the unbroken perverse outpourings of the Welsh Language Board and Welsh Nationalists.

Some months ago I happened upon a television programme which aimed to highlight the problems of promoting and expanding ancient languages and dialects - in this particular case the Northern Isles of

Scotland. As if the spread of the ubiquitous English was not enough, rural depopulation, resulting mainly from the movement of young people to towns and cities, had, it seemed, taken a severe toll on the local Celtic language to a point where it was almost extinct. Despite all official attempts to keep this crucial part of their culture alive the inevitable slide into oblivion beckoned. It took the foresight of a local islander to realise that it was these very bureaucratic schemes promoted by their Council which were destroying the culture rather than encouraging it's growth and development. By introducing free and informal introductions to the language, often based in one of the islander's cottages where a true community spirit could be cloned, the simple yet very effective scheme blossomed into a great success. Islanders and newcomers flocked to the doors to soak up the atmosphere, learn more about the history and culture of the island and take in a little of the language in relaxed surroundings. Prospering beyond anyone's wildest dreams and certainly to the astonishment yet delight of the authorities, who doubted success could be engineered from such small beginnings, the local language is almost off the 'danger list'. If only the Welsh could throw away their inhibitions, forget the English (as the English forget the Welsh!) and be as broadminded as the Scots and even the Japanese!

Sadly they have a long way to go as I have already found out. Etched in my memory is the Whist Drive I helped to organise for the Village School PTA and which was held in the Civic Hall of the local town. That night I was to learn two valuable lessons about Wales and it's indigenous population. Firstly, and of course most importantly, the Welsh are avid, nay almost professional Whist players who turn out in their hoards and take their game so seriously to the point where their very lives virtually depend on it. One could almost say it is more akin to a sub culture as bingo is to England and the chip buttie is to Yorkshire! Advice a plenty was offered to me that evening to assist me through their mystical world of whist. Both callers were Welsh as one would expect but even their English I found difficult to understand. As the evening progressed and 'warmed up' and players began to thoroughly enjoy themselves one of the callers, who happened to be a farmer and a governor of a nearby village school, began chatting to me about everything from beef cattle and BSE, education, abortion in sheep and low flying aircraft. I'm not sure even now after a short intervening period exactly how we turned the conversation round to the topic - a very thorny one as it turned out!

'Never remind them that they were defeated' he quietly whispered in my ear.

My immediate reaction was 'defeated by what?' and 'where?' and 'when?' and how it had anything to do with my few words of thanks I planned for the end of the evening. Confused but avoiding any mention of 'defeat' or 'English' in my vote of thanks it was not until I was home that I realised what my farmer friend had meant. He had been trying to warn me off attempting even a hint that the Welsh had been defeated by the English some 750 years ago! It's as bad if not worse than the Ulstermen and their 'hang ups' with the Battle of the Boyne. Who would have believed it!

The irony of the hostility and blinkered belligerence of many Welsh is that they appear not to realise how foolish they look to others and in particular the English. Unable it seems to laugh at themselves and ridiculously serious they have become the laughing stock of everyone around them. Not unlike the Irish, the Welsh harbour long and bitter memories which they are reluctant to pass over. Perhaps their stubbornness and independence is borne out of centuries of adversity and isolation, but frantic emotional declarations of 'Welshness', however well founded and well meaning, will not save a culture - it takes more than rhetoric. We may as well go all the way and set up our own Welsh army and Navy - a third of a frigate, half a tank, one jet and one helicopter and, of course, I must not forget the men on the ground with pitchforks and pikestaffs. What a farce!

I cannot wait to see the border posts complete with searchlights at the Severn Bridge with guards, leeks stuck in their lapels, singing 'Land of my Fathers' in the 'tongue', inspecting passports and taking tolls in Welsh pounds!

Hail Home Rule!

And the lights will go out all over Wales!

WHAT'S IN A NAME?

The Welsh Language Society is in the news once more.

This time it's not about burning down holiday cottages in the north of the principality or successfully curtailing the Queen's visit to open a university building at Aberystwyth but rather sounding off against one of our nearby colleges over it's apparent resistance to bend to their demands that it should become a Welsh language college and stop 'anglicising' it's students. Many will no doubt welcome what appears to be a slightly softer approach by Cymdeithas yr Iaith Gymraeg but no one should be fooled. The society's demands in this particular case would be backed by a 6 week campaign of direct action including disrupting college work and interference with the property - who said they had backed away from militant action? As if this were insufficient evidence as to the society's avowed intentions to rid Wales of 'anglicisation' I noted in a recent Welsh newspaper that they planned a demonstration against a famous premiership footballer and his equally famous popstar girlfriend who had dared to purchase a house in the Lleyn peninsula. Even the local Plaid Cymru Councillor rose to the occasion by insisting the couple should go on a Welsh learners course to become bilingual and failing their commitment to that they would not be welcome!

'Too many people' he said 'move to Wales without appreciating they are moving to somewhere that has a different culture'.

True, it is a different culture, but it is not a nation! It is but a principality and part of the kingdom where tolerance should be shown and everyone have the freedom to choose what language they wish to speak - be it English or Celtic. When all said and done there are considerable differences in dialect, pronunciation and even words between North and South Wales - this was made very apparent recently at our local village school. An argument between a teacher and a parent literally turned on the individual interpretation between the local villagers and those living in the county town some 12 miles distant. The parent was staunchly local whilst the teacher, who lived in the county town, had been taught Welsh at the local college. Mayhem reigned! Why the Welsh have to be so unyielding and uncompromising on the pronunciation of their language is a total anomaly when there are so many variations within the same street!

Each dialect is, if the truth be known, a gloriously complex mix of various 'tongues' that have developed naturally over the centuries and been passed from generation to generation. They are not unlike the diverse 'language' of traditional or vernacular buildings where the glory and interest lies in their very own variations and idiosyncrasies that are inextricably linked with their own community and neighbourhood. Sadly very few people these days notice or care for these distinctly local traditions in building but yet strangely and slavishly follow the spoken word almost to the point of being pedantic. True, our dialects in language are precious and should be protected wherever possible as part of an overall British heritage but the Welsh intolerance is almost beyond belief. There can be few places in the kingdom where it is insisted that all written documents from public organisations must be produced in both English and Welsh at vast expense to the 'man in the street'. Has anyone ever asked him if he would prefer that money to be spent on the health and education services? I doubt it! Has anyone ever calculated the time and costs involved in using interpreters for this highly dubious service? Bilingualism has even invaded our roads and public buildings but to what end? Surely the Welsh dialect, or language as the diehard nationalists prefer to call it, should stand in it's own right without being forced on the population at every street corner and in every facet of life. Most people in the street, staggering though it may be to the indigenous Welsh, have little interest or deep feelings for the Welsh language and are just intent on earning an 'honest crust' and keeping the bank manager off their back. Does it really matter whether your pronunciation is correct or not - a couple of miles down the road the pronunciation may well be acceptable and the word may even mean something totally different! In my travels and sojourns across the kingdom, whether it be in gritty Yorkshire and County Durham or the softer almost sleepy depths of Norfolk and Suffolk I have never been corrected on my pronunciation of their dialect and heaven knows it was hard enough many a time to understand what on earth they were saying!

Wherever I might be I have come to enjoy the dialects with all their wrinkles and creases and peacefully pass the time of day with the locals even though I would be the first to admit it often sounds a load of 'mumbo jumbo!' I wouldn't dare to comment on their pronunciation - they've had years of experience!

Coming from a region of the kingdom that has it's own peculiar and diverse dialects I was reminded one glorious summer evening by a hardy old Fenland character, whilst sitting outside a country pub called the 'Mad Cat', that even the locals couldn't pronounce some village names correctly. After analysing at some length the happenings of the previous evening when the Mad Cat darts team had seen off one of the high flying townie squads and no doubt downed much ale in celebration, the old local asked me if I knew the names of a couple of villages some 20 or 30 miles distant.

'Yew know Bozeat and Farcet?'

'Of course - why do you ask?' I replied.

'Well this 'ere lot 'us arguin' aboot how yew speak it'. The discussion on pronunciation continued for a considerable time in a light - hearted and jovial manner over pints of bitter, the pair of us being joined eventually by several other locals. No vast conclusions were arrived at and the conversation drifted into oblivion until the old gentleman suddenly came to life on the subject again.

'Wots it matter anyway how yew sez it?'

Those were his last words on the subject as he lifted his weary and weather beaten frame from the old settle. He had a point – life's too short to worry over such trifles.

C'est la vie or rather Hynny yw bywyd!

Footnote: I recently saw BBC's Countryfile Programme that centred on the Lleyn peninsula in Wales. Apart from talking about the Welsh Language Centre, John Craven raised the issue of the doubling in size of Pwllheli's marina. A member of the Welsh Language Society vehemently opposed the extension stating 'Its too English a development'. He also complained that the local populace of 900, of whom he declared some 80% spoke Welsh, were invaded by almost 25000 'English speaking' tourists in the season. He considered this was unacceptable despite the fact that it provided employment and brought £22m into the local economy! It is so sad to see such people attacking 'outsiders' who have the guts to plan and fund such developments – the indigenous Welsh population don't seem to like seeing 'outsiders' being successful in their back yard! Surely the Welsh Language Society do not really consider they can prevent 'non Welsh born' and 'non 'Welsh speakers' setting up business, spending their money and buying properties in Wales? The Human Rights Act may have some flaws but this does enshrine the right to speak whatever language you wish, buy whatever property you desire and sell to whoever offers you the asking price – be they Indian, Polish or Russian!

IX

TIME
TO
REFLECT

TIME TO REFLECT

Curled up on the old Moroccan rug in front of a roaring log fire I gazed into the dancing and ever changing colours of the flames as they sped skywards up the chimney and pondered on what had been and what was yet to come.

I had come a long way since my first years in a Fenland village when summers seemed one endless round of enjoyment and winters froze you to the bone. Both countryside and society have changed immeasurably and certainly beyond anyone's expectations in the space of near 50 years - but not always for the best. Events and life have moved on at a mind boggling speed and far too fast for either you or I to comprehend. To many living in today's 'fast lane' it may all appear immaterial as they strive for more money and creature comforts fed by an insatiable thirst to live, build and buy bigger and better. How would they have coped 50 years ago?

True, we are healthier, eat better and apparently are happier. But at the back of my mind is a nagging doubt that grows ever greater as the years go by. Are we in better 'mind and spirit' than in my childhood days when my grandparents were alive? Life then was a struggle but yet wonderfully enjoyable within family and community circles which thrived to the benefit of all - each knew everyone else in town, village or remote hamlet and there was always a helping hand at harvest, lambing or at times of personal crises. It's a sombre fact to reflect on the current 'health' of the kingdom - poorer in 'mind and spirit', beset with troubles and with a potentially increasing gulf between rich and poor, the 'haves' and the 'have nots', which no one can either attempt to tackle or be bothered to care about. Life is projected at such an hectic pace that many are left in its wake with no chance of survival and little or no support from individuals or community. We are fast becoming an uncaring society.

Red hot ash from one of the oak logs falls onto the old stone hearth and temporarily stirs me from my distant thoughts. As the intensity of the fire begins to fade and the heat subsides I think back to happy times spent in that cathedral city close to the Fens. It was a time of being educated and reminded, time and time again, that they were the 'best years of your life'. How we used to groan every time we were reminded but how true those words really were! Apart from the old city centre with it's 'legal quarter', the Cathedral, St. John's Parish Church and the Guildhall it is now unrecognisable. The old place has been consumed in the space of thirty years by vast swathes of development and a network of motorway roads - something I could never have imagined as a grammar school pupil. The pace of life in Peterborough is almost as bad as that of London - I couldn't contemplate spending a day in the 'big smoke' let alone living there. And I thought that living and working in London 25 years ago was hectic! Bath, where I once sought refuge, is rapidly catching up whilst suffering even more from the deluges of home made and foreign tourists intent on 'clocking up' yet another tourist 'hot spot'. Not even the Cotswolds are immune from these pressures when I was firmly of the belief that they had reached saturation point many years ago. To compound the already frighteningly mad and impossible lifestyle, material conformity in the very buildings we live in is 'infecting' everywhere you travel. It matters little whether you are in Somerset or Dorset since to all intents and purposes you may as well be in Sunderland, Southampton, Huntingdon or Uttoxeter! To be denied the very sense of place and belonging, a most personal contentment and aspiration, is just too much. There are, surprisingly, a few isolated pockets of 'non conformity' but they are becoming fewer by the day. Wales, and in particular the isolated countryside of the Brecon Beacons, the Cambrian Mountains and the rugged West Coast, retains remnants of untouched glory and magnificence. But even in our sojourn in a tiny West Wales village the community has not been spared the spreading 'cancer' that feeds across the land.

I throw another log onto the dying embers as I admit in my own mind that not everything is despondency, sadness and failure and that there are still rays of light that glimmer amidst the fast gathering clouds of the oncoming evening. Across the land lies a richness and variety of life, landscape and legend which is unique, fulfilling and refreshing if we did but bother to recognise and enjoy it, having stripped away the modern over mantle. On a recent visit to my old cathedral city of Peterborough I stood and gazed across flood meadows, full to overflowing from the recent heavy rains and reflecting stumps of ancient gnarled willows that lined the banks. The ancient cathedral and it's welcoming group of monastic buildings stood guard like a sentinel over the rain drenched, mist laden land and was joined, as if in celebration of the advancement of our beleaguered society, by stark outlines of office blocks, flats and even the football stadium and it's floodlight pylons. How those Norman invaders must have quaked at the very sight of those imposing ecclesiastical structures silhouetted against an angry evening winter sky - today's transient, impersonal and secular edifices would hardly raise a flicker of emotion, fear or wonder!

I couldn't help but wonder what the old Fen farm labourer was doing with his prized crop of sugar beet and if that weather beaten Fenman still supplied the Abbey Tea Rooms with his luscious honey. What became of those old fen characters at the Mad Cat public house? Maybe they are still lifting a pint or two and arguing over the pronunciation of some long forgotten fenland community in that great public house in the sky.

Wales - land of mists, legends and evocative landscapes - has yet to satisfy my search for a spirit that will last and outlive all else that is. Peaceful, passionately introvert and patriotic, it remains a temporary haven.

Traditions may come and go but the Fen spirit remains true and steadfast - there is nothing to match it.

Born a Fenman - always a Fenman!

It is still forever home.

PHOTOGRAPHIC NOTES

As a self taught photographer who thankfully took the opportunity to take photography as a 'second subject' whilst studying for a qualification in Architecture in the 1960's I have admired and taken inspiration from many photographers – amongst them Rob Talbot, Andrew Lawson, Tony Evans, Andrew Butler, Mike Read, David Boag and not least, of course, the late Lord Lichfield.

Some 40 years ago as an Architectural student 'ploughing' through a 7 year course, I invested much of my winter and summer vacation work earnings in a 'heavyweight' 35mm SLR camera and standard lens – a Hanimex SL and 1.7 Hanimar lens – for use on dissertations and theses. I considered my equipment 'state of the art' and it certainly proved a workhorse over the years. The black and white photographs included in this book of Peterborough city centre in the late 60's ahead of New Town 'regeneration' were taken on the Hanimex. Sadly as a student I did not take sufficient account of weather conditions, still the controlling factor in the 21st century despite the 'up market' electronic and digital equipment. Many of the 'regeneration' photographs were taken in appalling weather and atrocious light conditions. The Hanimex, although now hopelessly out dated, is still working and able to produce excellent photographs.

Now I am a freelance photographer specialising in the built heritage, landscapes, contemporary images based on 'seas, sand and rivers' and rail transport. Some of the photographs I have included in this book date from the very first days of being a freelance when I had first invested in a Canon 35mm SLR camera and was using Ilford FP4 as a trial. My attention then to suitable weather conditions and filter use was, I admit, not as sharp as it should have been. I often find autumn and winter in early morning or late evening are the best times for photography – when the light is soft. It is a logistical nightmare to be at every location you need to be when conditions are perfect – some scenes are thus captured in not so perfect light or are sadly missed out altogether. As I now live just 20 miles from the West Wales coast, Towy estuary and Carmarthen Bay I find a link to the BBC Weather Service, giving local details for 5 days ahead, invaluable, although even the BBC can get it wrong! Quite often it can be perfect in our valley but thick mist and low cloud on the coast!

Now the Hanimex is retired I rely on a Canon EOS30 and a Canon EOS20D which give me a pleasant mix of film and digital formats. As for lenses I regularly use the Canon 18-55 USM, 28-105 Mk.2 USM and 75-300 USM. I find the 18-55 lens very useful in 'tight' situations despite potential parallax problems and the creation of small spaces seeming larger whilst the 28-105, at it's top end, is useful in bringing elements of the composition closer together. These lenses offer me sufficient flexibility in the wide range of work I am asked to undertake. Films used include Ilford FP4, and XP2 and Fuji 200 Superia whilst memory cards for the digital camera are San Disk Ultra 2. It goes without saying that I always use a tripod. I still use my trusty 30 year old Cullman although I must admit a recent three day session over railway ballast seems to have almost brought it to it's knees! The medium weight Manfrotto is now the mainstay for my work.

All photographs are the authors unless otherwise duly acknowledged.

BIBLIOGRAPHY

Betjeman, John. *Collins Guide to English Parish Churches.* Collins 1959

Clare, John. *Extracts from Poems.* Curtis Brown Group, London on behalf of Eric Robinson

Darby H C. *The Medieval Fenland.* David and Charles 1940. Republished Cambridge University Press 1974

Davies, Martin. *Save the last of the magic.* Crown Print 1991

Ditchfield P H. *The Charm of the English Village.* Bracken Books 1985

Evans, Tony & Green, Lycett Candida. *English Villages.* Weidenfeld & Nicolson 1982

Gunton, Simon. *The History of the Church of Peterborough.* 1685

Hill, Michael & Birch, Sally. *Cotswold Stone Homes.* Alan Sutton 1994

Jekyll G & Jones S R. *Old English Household Life.* B T Batsford 2nd ed. rev. 1944

Laws B & Butler A. *Old English Farmhouses.* Collins and Brown. 1992

Lowe, Jeremy. *Welsh Country Workers Housing 1775-1875.* National Museum of Wales 1993

Mee, Arthur. *The Lake Counties,* King's England. Hodder & Stoughton 1949

Mee, Arthur. *Northamptonshire,* King's England. Hodder & Stoughton 1949

Mee, Arthur. *Cambridgeshire,* King's England. Hodder & Stoughton 1965

Mee, Arthur. *Bedford & Huntingdon*, King's England. Hodder & Stoughton 1939

Mee, Arthur. *Lincolnshire*, King's England. Hodder & Stoughton 1949

Moore, Kenneth A. *The Vanishing Vernacular Series*, Carmarthenshire Life Magazine 1996 - 1997

Perry C, Gore A & Fleming L. *Old English Villages.* Phoenix Illustrated 1977

Pevsner, Sir Nikolaus. *Cambridgeshire.* Penguin 1970

Pevsner, Sir Nikolaus. *Northamptonshire.* Penguin 1961

Pevsner, Sir Nikolaus. *Bedfordshire, Huntingdonshire and Peterborough.* Penguin 1968

Pevsner, Sir Nikolaus / revised by Enid Radcliffe. *Essex.* Penguin 1965

Pevsner, Sir Nikolaus. *North Somerset and Bristol.* Penguin 1958

Pevsner, Sir Nikolaus/ co author John Harris. *Lincolnshire.* Penguin 1964

Pevsner, Sir Nikolaus / co author David Verney. *Gloucestershire : The Cotswolds.* Penguin 1991

Pevsner, Sir Nikolaus. *Cumberland and Westmorland.* Penguin 1997

Pevsner, Sir Nikolaus. *North Lancashire.* Penguin 1969

Readers Digest. *Folklore, Myths and Legends of Britain.* Hodder & Stoughton 1973

Redhead, Brian. *Months in the Country.* Ebury Press 1992

Royal Commission on Historic Monuments {England}. *Huntingdonshire* 1926

Smith, Peter. *Houses of the Welsh Countryside.* RCAHMW / HMSO 1988

Storey, Edward. *Call it a Summer Country*. Hale 1978

Storey, Edward. *Portrait of The Fen Country*. Hale 1978

Storey, Edward. *The Solitary Landscape*. Victor Gollanz 1975

Storey, Edward. *Letters from the Fens*. Hale 1998

Storey, Edward. *In Fen Country Heaven*. Hale 1996

Storey, Edward. *Fen Boy First*. Hale 1992

Talbot R & Whiteman R. *The English Lakes*. Phoenix Illustrated 1997

Tebbs H F. *Peterborough*. Oleander Press 1979

Vaughan - Thomas, Winford. *The Countryside Companion*. Hutchinson, Webb and Bower 1979

Vesey - Fitzgerald, Brian. *The British Countryside in Pictures*. Odhams. No date

Wiliam, Eurwyn. *Welsh Long Houses*. University of Wales Press/ National Museum of Wales 1992

Wiliam, Eurwyn. *Home made Homes*. University of Wales Press/ National Museum of Wales 1993